The
ASSISTANT OFFICERS
A Practical Guide

Richard Johnson

Lewis Masonic

First published 2002

ISBN 0 85318 228 0

Published by Lewis Masonic

an imprint of Ian Allan Publishing Ltd,
Hersham, Surrey KT12 4RG.
Printed by Ian Allan Printing Ltd,
Hersham, Surrey KT12 4RG.

Explanation of front cover
Top left: Inner Guard's jewel
Top right: Deacon's modern jewel
Centre: Tyler's jewel
Bottom left and right: Sun and moon Deacons' jewels (some of the older lodges,
pre-United Grand Lodge, are permitted to retain their original Deacons' jewels,
and these and the Mercury jewels are further explained in the introduction to the
chapters on the Deacons' duties)

Contents

Preface

This book is written to guide the Assistant Officers of a lodge – the junior ranks of the regular Officers – through the range of duties that they will be expected to perform during their year of office. Often these positions are filled by Masons who have relatively recently joined the Craft, and some explanatory information may be very helpful to them in amplifying the instructions contained in their lodge rituals. This book covers the basic ceremonial to be performed within the lodge, and outlines some of the additional duties that may be expected of these Officers. It also briefly describes the history of the various offices and how they originally arose in the early lodges, which may help to put into perspective why certain actions are required at different times in the ritual. But most of all it is written to help ensure that the Mason is prepared for the range of duties annexed to each office as he embarks on his progression towards the Chair of his lodge.

This book, however, is not written as an exhaustive guide to every possible variation that exists in the Craft ritual across the over 7,000 lodges that operate within the English Constitution. This would be an unnecessarily repetitious method of explaining the duties of each office. It is recognised that each lodge has its own traditions, some retained for over two centuries of working and some couched in a language specific to that lodge, and no Director of Ceremonies wants any member of his lodge trying to adopt new concepts that are foreign to its modus operandi. Rather this book should be read

4

in conjunction with the lodge ritual, and only as a basis for general reference has the Emulation ritual been alluded to in each section of the book. Among the other rituals adopted by some lodges are Taylor's, Logic, Sussex, Oxford, West End, Stability, Revised, the Craft Guide and the Complete Workings. Still further rituals exist in the Bristol lodges, and also in Shakspere Lodge and Pellipar Lodge (Cartwright's).

Even in these exhaustive rituals there are times when the ritual book does not indicate how a certain action is performed or if any words are used. Each lodge will have adopted a stratagem for coping with these apparent blanks, and the young Mason is recommended to check with the Director and Assistant Director of Ceremonies if he needs any guidance to ensure that he maintains the lodge traditions. In other cases the methodology of the ritual has had to be slightly revised because of the geography of the lodge room and furniture contained therein. For the new Mason's further education he should endeavour to attend the practice meetings held by the lodge and witness exactly how things are done, and better still he should volunteer to perform parts of the ceremonies so that he gains a feel for how each ceremony flows. The Director of Ceremonies and his Assistant will doubtless be encouraged to see such enthusiasm, and will hopefully begin to reward the volunteer with formal tasks that are within his capability.

Having noted the preceding, the book is written to give the Assistant Officers an added degree of confidence about their work and their roles in the lodge. Above all, it is hoped that this will help the Officer to enjoy his Masonry more, and indeed there is very little value belonging to an organisation in which you do not enjoy participating. However, as many experienced Masons have found previously, the degree of confidence and enjoyment in carrying out any role in the lodge is greatly increased by making sure you are as prepared as possible for the work. This may not necessarily mean attending every practice meeting, although these are primarily to help any Officer or member discover where he needs to give extra attention to detail, but it will mean studying the ritual that your lodge operates in order to ensure that you know when, where and hopefully why the ritual proceeds as it does. The old adage is 'practice makes perfect', and without it you may not be able to perform your prescribed duties with as much satisfaction to yourself and your lodge as you might otherwise be capable of doing.

Introduction

‘And how many Assistant Officers are there in the lodge?’ These are the words spoken at the start of every lodge meeting, by the Master to the Senior Warden. In reply the Inner Guard and the Deacons are noted, along with the Tyler or Outer Guard.

The three inside the lodge effectively work as a junior team, each answering to one of the Principal Officers: the Inner Guard to the Junior Warden, the Junior Deacon to the Senior Warden, and the Senior Deacon to the Master. As the progression through a lodge often includes holding these offices in turn, it seems sensible to describe their duties together in the one book. In some lodges the Tyler is also a progressive office and in others it is not, but in any case the Tyler and Inner Guard work together as a sub-unit and their duties are also perhaps usefully detailed alongside each other for comparison and reference.

The other office to which junior brethren often find themselves appointed is that of Steward, and the path to the Master's chair will often begin with this position. In large lodges there may be many Stewards and a waiting list of brethren to join them, while in smaller ones an initiate may find himself almost immediately thrust into these duties. This book, aimed at helping the junior brethren, therefore includes Stewards with the other Assistant Officers, and your early taste of helping to organise and run the lodge for the benefit of its brethren and visitors will include many if not all of the above-mentioned offices.

Interestingly several of the early lodges used to operate without any of these Assistant Officers except for the Tyler, and from their records they did so for many years at a time when lodge memberships were quite small. However, as Freemasonry developed after the 17th Century – firstly under the Premier Grand Lodge and thereafter also under the Antients' and then the United Grand Lodges – it became normal practice to include the Assistants in the standard list of Officers, and most lodge summons will detail all of the office-holders. Perhaps the incorporation of some of the Irish traditions into the English lodges during the mid-18th Century, and the fact that there were several military lodges where the custom in the Army was to have junior officers reporting to senior officers, assisted in this increase in the number of Officers operating in a lodge. On one hand we are told in the ritual that seven make a perfect lodge, whilst the Book of Constitutions, paragraph 104 sets out who are the regular Officers: the Master, Wardens, Deacons, Inner Guard, Tyler, Treasurer and Secretary, making nine in total. This can reduce to eight, if the Tyler is not a member of the lodge but is elected as a non-member to that office.

The Book of Constitutions continues by stating that the Master shall appoint an Almoner and Charity Steward as additional Officers, a relatively recent insistence, but each regular Officer can also take on one additional office, so the minimum legal lodge membership remains at eight. The remaining six further additional Officers on a lodge listing – Chaplain, Director of Ceremonies and his Assistant, Organist, Assistant Secretary and Steward(s) – are optional, and again the regular Officers can take on double roles if required. Undoubtedly a lodge runs more smoothly with a healthy complement of Officers, and occupying the assistant ranks gives each junior some useful experience of Masonic work before undertaking the senior roles, as well as giving them the chance to show that they can cope with the different responsibilities of the various offices.

The Steward

This may be your first appointment in your lodge and, because normally you are part of a small team working alongside other lodge members, there is plenty of useful advice on what is required of you from your fellow Stewards or from the other brethren who have passed through that office.

Some Background to the Office

The history of this office is quite interesting. In the small lodges of the 18th Century the Junior Warden was the Steward of the lodge, and he is reminded of this fact at every installation meeting when he is addressed as the 'ostensible Steward of the lodge'. In those early days before Treasurers were appointed, the Junior Warden also looked after the finances of the lodge with regard to paying the bills for the meals and liquor, etc., after lodge meetings. In fact he had many roles within a lodge, and probably welcomed the idea of being able to call on the assistance of Stewards when these began to be more widely appointed. It was in the 18th Century at major festivals that the additional appointment of event Stewards began to be introduced to help with the organisation, by assisting with the sales of dining tickets and the income therefrom, and also looking after the attendees on the day. Special jewels were struck for them to wear, a practice that is still seen today when the different Provinces hold charity festivals, etc.

Whilst it may still nominally be the duty of the Junior Warden to ensure that visitors are properly attended to, more often than not it is now customary that he delegates this part of his former responsibilities to the Treasurer and a team of lodge Stewards to assist at festive boards. If the duties of Steward include the replenishment of wine on the tables for visitors, then it is the Treasurer who will sanction when this occurs and to what extent, although the Stewards will also be waiting on the tables if any

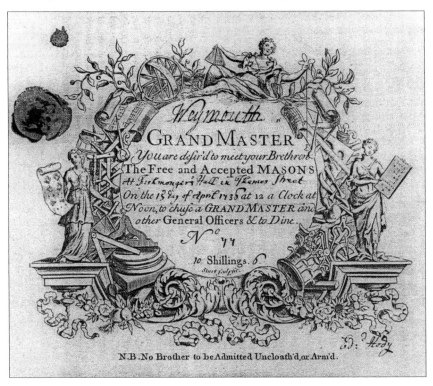

Admission ticket to the 1736 Grand Festival, bearing the signature of one of the Grand Stewards, Dr Edward Hody. In the early days of festivals, the Stewards were expected to make up any shortfall of income over expenditure, and as the Stewards did not set the admission price it was soon found that less and less volunteers were coming forward to be a Steward. Fortunately for the current lodge Stewards, this practice was quickly abandoned!

member or visitor wants to place a personal order for a round of drinks for his friends. The Junior Warden will in many lodges propose a toast to the visitors, which appears to be the only remnant left over from his earlier duties at the festive board.

An Outline of the Duties

As a Steward you will have been advised of your essential duties when you were invested at the installation meeting. These include ensuring visitors are properly accommodated, for seating and for refreshments, helping with the collection of any monies as directed, and assisting the other lodge Officers as appropriate. The office jewel, being a cornucopia or horn of plenty, indicates that you will be involved with the supply of victuals at the festive board. Each lodge has its own modus operandi, and from being an initiate you may have noticed how some lodge members seemed to be more active at the meals than others. Some lodges appoint a Senior Steward who will co-ordinate the efforts of his team, and he may be an older member of the lodge or the longest-serving Steward who will be moving on to higher office soon. Normally the Director of Ceremonies and Treasurer will also be directly involved at the festive boards, with the formalities and running order to be observed and also with the lodge finances to safeguard, so you may at times be asked to assist either of these Officers. If it is your custom for raffles to be conducted, you may also be asked to assist the Charity Steward in selling tickets and other items during the meals.

Also at the installation you will be advised that 'your regular and early/punctual attendance (at meetings) will be the best proof of your zeal and attachment'. Lodge meetings and festive boards are usually run to a schedule, so that the agenda is fully covered within a reasonable timescale and members can depart without missing any important items. These days there is not the same reliance on public transport as in bygone days, when missing the last train or bus could cause serious problems. The lodge was indeed fortunate if the driver sympathised with members leaving the festive board a little late, and there are stories in Cumbria for example of train drivers reporting 'sheep on the line' as an excuse to wait for lodge members to complete their meals and speeches quickly. This was, however, in an era when the strict observance of timetables was not as mandatory as today, at least with the last train of the evening, so it is perhaps a moot point whether or not local communities are served better nowadays than when some flexibility was perhaps unofficially tolerated.

The prompt attention of Stewards in coping with the smooth running of the festive board helps to ensure it is efficiently managed. You may have left the lodge early to prepare the dining room, perhaps setting out place names to the table plan. At well-attended meetings you may need to carry some chairs from the lodge room to the dining room. Often you will be ensuring that brethren are not thirsty, and there are normally several toasts to honour, so a swift replenishment of glasses before the first or second toast of the evening is always a good idea. You may also be required to assist in serving the different courses of the meal, ensuring that the Master is served first, and in collecting the plates at the completion of each course, although many lodges employ catering staff so that all brethren can enjoy their meals in relative peace. In some premises you may also be called on to serve behind the bar, either for general consumption or for senior Masons at a major lodge event such as an installation. In such cases there will be several people to help you find your feet, either fellow Stewards or members who have served in that role previously.

The other meetings that you will be expected to attend will be the practices or Lodges of Instruction. The Master and Director of Ceremonies will be on the look-out from time to time for someone to substitute for an Officer who cannot be present at the next lodge meeting, and they obviously want to be able to select someone who is a reliable attendee. At many practice meetings there will be the opportunity for juniors to undertake part or all of the duties of the different offices in the lodge, and this is a useful way of being introduced gently to performing part of the lodge ritual instead of being only a spectator. Some lodges with several juniors may even have an occasional lodge meeting where juniors occupy the regular offices, perhaps Senior Deacon downwards, and perform the full ceremony, although these days with falling memberships the more frequent replacement of the regular Officers is on a Past Masters' Night. Hopefully as many members as possible will be encouraged to participate in the ceremonies because, when someone has been keen enough to become a Mason these days, placing him onto an extensive Stewards' list for several years only to watch the proceedings but not take any part seems to be a recipe for killing off that initial enthusiasm.

So this is your opportunity to flex your wings, and the lodge will much prefer to find a volunteer rather than having to twist people's arms to perform the various items included in the ceremonies. Most lodges will be careful not to be too demanding of juniors until they have the necessary confidence to work in a full lodge meeting – and believe me, however calm you are at home or in the practice room, the first full formal lodge meeting in which you participate definitely has a different feel to it. Despite this, you should remember that every Mason – including even the most accomplished ritualist – has started off in this way, and there is a Chinese proverb that the most difficult part of any journey is the first step. One item of ritual that is frequently delegated to juniors is the explanation of the working tools, so you might begin by trying to commit these to memory – and the extended version of the Fellowcraft's tools is possibly one of the best pieces of prose that we have in the ritual book.

Having assisted in the running of the lodge and festive boards, and possibly having been called on to perform some items of ritual inside the lodge room, you are now ready to move into one of the more formal offices in the lodge.

Andrew Montgomery, 'Garder of ye Grand Lodge', 1738.

The Tyler

It seems sad in a way that the office of Tyler is sometimes occupied by a junior brother, although it is thought that in several older lodges the most junior Entered Apprentice was traditionally deputed to act as that Officer. This seems a little odd for someone who needed to recognise all lodge members as well as prepare candidates for all of the ceremonies. It is possible that for a first degree ceremony the junior Entered Apprentice could be delegated for the job of being within the lodge (ie as Inner Guard) and opening the door to admit visitors, latecomers and candidates for initiation, but obviously he could not continue in that post for a higher degree than he had already undergone himself. In any case, regardless of history, the Book of Constitutions has for a long time decreed that the Tyler has to be at least a Master Mason.

You may have completed several items of ritual on the floor of the lodge as a junior and/or a Steward and, just when you have become familiar with the layout and workings of the lodge, you end up outside the door. However, several lodges appoint Past Masters to this office, and of those some have this as the next responsibility for a retiring Immediate Past Master, who tends to be somewhat at a loose end after two years in the East of the lodge room. Other lodges who meet together in one Masonic Hall can sometimes appoint a Tyler to serve most or all of the lodges, so that every member can enjoy the meeting from within. In such circumstances the Book of Constitutions, paragraph 113 is quite clear in that a non-member of a lodge as Tyler must be elected at the appropriate lodge meeting prior to the installation.

Some Background to the Office

This office is obviously one of the most important in the lodge. At the lodge business meeting prior to the installation the Master Elect and Treasurer are balloted for, and in many lodges so is the Tyler, making this office something special. In fact if the Tyler is not a member of the lodge he has to be elected formally, whereas the Master can appoint one of his members to that office without payment. Some Tylers perform that duty for several lodges and, in the early days of Grand Lodge Anderson's *Book of Constitutions* of 1723 decreed that the Tyler should not be a member of the lodge, perhaps so that all of the members could discuss matters freely within the lodge room.

The word 'Tyler' is derived from the trades' guilds to which skilled craftsmen belonged, and people who laid roof tiles/tyles as the outermost weather-cladding of a building were associated with other building trades – carpenters, bricklayers, plasterers, and masons. As the trade secrets were jealously guarded, it would be the norm for a guard to be posted at the door of the meeting room to prevent anybody from overhearing the discussions or training and thereby learning some of the skills. As this was the outermost defence of their confidential meetings, the guarding of the door became known as 'tyling', although doorkeeper or guard was the more usual expression adopted in early lodges. The first reference to 'Tyler' for the title of the office within Grand Lodge appeared in its minutes during 1732, although there had been some earlier references to that word in private lodges just before then.

In the lodges of the early 18th Century, the Tyler was the first Officer to be paid for his services. Apart from his duties at the door of the lodge, his other duties included delivering the summons to the members, for which he maintained the lodge list of members' addresses in the days before Secretaries and Treasurers. He would also keep an up-to-date list of other lodges meeting in the area that were approved by Grand Lodge and, with spurious lodges springing up after the publication of several Masonic disclosures, this was a necessary safeguard for the brethren in the 18th Century.

Several lodge records note that the Tyler was paid a remuneration by every candidate at each ceremony, and joining members also paid the Tyler for their personal details to be entered into the lodge list of members. Some lodges also note that the Tyler's meal and some liquid refreshment was paid for, or an allowance given to cover these costs. Many of the early brethren agreed to pay their lodge subscriptions at every meeting, rather than the annual levy in common practice today, and obviously those staying for the meal would also pay the cost of the festive board. In this sense the Tyler was supporting the Junior Warden of the lodge, on whom usually fell the responsibility of paying the innkeeper for the food and drink consumed at the festive board.

The 1737 by-laws of Friendship Lodge No. 6, for example, outlined the duties and remuneration thus:

'The Doorkeeper is to have Twelvepence every time of his Attendance. He is never to be off Duty in Lodge Hours, nor be anyhow negligent or remiss in it. He is to take care of the Clothing of the Members, and Utensils of the Lodge. He is to offer a List to be subscribed by the Members as Visitors shall call for, to cause them (being vouched for) to enter their names in his List, with ye particular Lodge to which they belong, and set down who the persons are that recommend them. He is also before their admission to receive Twelvepence apiece from such Visitors, and to produce ye said List and receipts to the Master or Wardens before the Lodge is closed. He is to keep the Key of the Apron Box, etc., and be ready with it always in good time; or failing in any of these, he shall lose his pay for the Night.'

As lodges developed, so did the role of the Tyler. In some lodges with large memberships there were appointed an 'Upper' Tyler and an 'Under' Tyler, and in one or two lodges even an additional Assistant Tyler was appointed. The duties would be split and, where there were the two brethren, one would attend to delivering the summons for the meeting and the other would attend to the preparation of the lodge room. It may be from this doubling up on the Tyler's duties that the Inner Guard's role developed, and indeed some of the older lodges have referred in their minutes to the second Officer as the 'Inner Tyler'.

Another aspect of the early Tyler's duties was to prepare the lodge room for the ceremony to be conducted, including the etching or chalking of the symbols that would be explained to the candidate during the evening. These were the precursors of the tracing cloths or boards that are now almost universally used in lodge rooms, and which have eliminated the potential requirement that a Tyler had to be a reasonably good artist. This depiction of the Masonic symbols in the centre of the lodge room floor also provides a good reason for traditionally squaring round the sides of the lodge, in order to avoid damaging the artwork previously completed. The first mention of a tracing cloth to remove this requirement for artistic dexterity was in 1737, after which several lodges rapidly followed suit. The Tyler is still expected to assist in preparing the lodge room, by laying out the furniture, ensuring the lodge banner is visible, etc., but this is normally performed in conjunction with the Director of Ceremonies.

The Tyler's post is outside the door of the lodge room. For some early lodge premises this actually meant outside the building, and as well as the sword (not always permitted in public) the Tyler was given a heavy coat or cape to keep himself relatively warm and dry during the cold and often damp winter months. In this position the Tyler's job was to keep away any possible eavesdroppers, and in some lodges the punishment for being caught by the Tyler was for the culprit to be stood for 20 minutes under the downspout from the roof in heavy rain, with the water pouring in at the neck and out through his shoes! After the first one or two 'arrests', word would spread around the locality fairly quickly that this punishment was best avoided, and anyway you could probably not hear clearly what was going on inside the lodge room for your pains. Other lodges also had special hats for the Tyler, the hairy ones alluded to in some lodges being especially useful on cold winter's nights, and dress hats for formal processions.

Gradually as new offices were introduced into the lodges – the Inner Guard, Secretary, and Treasurer in particular – several of the Tyler's once wide-ranging duties have been taken over by them. Apart from his ceremonial entrances to make up an incoming or outgoing procession, the Tyler is now entrusted with the first job given him by the craft guilds, to guard the outside of the lodge door as well as preparing candidates for the different ceremonies. Certainly if it is the lodge practice to make the Tyler's office a progressive one, you will nowadays be expected to concentrate only on the ritual aspects rather than on all of the other former responsibilities.

An Outline of the Duties

Your essential duties are again summarised in the address given to you at the installation. These include the announcement of visitors or members, the preparation of candidates, and responding to the knocks of the Inner Guard. Many lodge rooms have a small flap built into the door in order for you to communicate with the Inner Guard, so that you do not give the knocks announcing that someone seeks admission at a most inappropriate time. Whether or not you have this facility, you should try to establish an understanding with your fellow Officer in order to operate effectively. The jewel of your office is a single sword, which has an obvious allusion to the traditional weaponry of that bygone era with which the early Tylers were armed, and that for ceremonial purposes they still are.

Preparing the Lodge Room

As noted above, it may be part of your duties to assist the Director of Ceremonies in laying out the lodge room, and you may be given a set of keys to the cupboard or container where your lodge regalia is stored. Your punctual attendance would be much appreciated, as very few Directors of Ceremonies like to set up the lodge room at the last minute or when visitors are already arriving for the meeting. You will have often heard the adage 'a place for everything, and everything in its place', and this is true for laying out the lodge furniture. Your lodge may have a checklist of items to be attended to, but if it does not then you may be advised to make some notes for the first occasions on which you are assisting in this preparation.

One day it may come in useful when you become Director of Ceremonies, and you will learn that older brethren dislike the lodge layout to be changing markedly with each new Director of Ceremonies!

W Bro David Russell, PPrSGD (E. Lancs) with the coat and hat as worn by the Tyler in the Lodge of Tranquillity No 274, Rawtenstall (E. Lancs) at installation meetings. In the early lodges the Tyler could be stood outside the lodge building, normally without his ceremonial sword, and a thick coat would be very useful for the cold winter nights.

You should especially ensure the Tyler's book or attendance sheets are available at the lodge room door, so that members and visitors can sign in on arrival, even if the Secretary customarily brings the appropriate items with him. He may be distracted on other matters, and technically it is your book – another throwback to the early days of Tyler's duties. By the Tyler's book there may also be cards placed for visitors to complete in order to ease your job of announcing them to the Inner Guard, and for him to announce them formally in the lodge. The other item to watch for is placing the working tools at the correct position in the lodge room, and this depends from where the explanation is customarily delivered in your lodge during each degree ceremony. The checklist of items at the end of this book may be of assistance to you as a start, but remember to alter it to accommodate your lodge traditions.

The Book may be only opened at one place for all ceremonies, or it may be opened at different specified positions for each degree and you should check that, if the Book is shared by several lodges, your traditions are preserved. In some ways the constant reopening of the Book at different positions for the three degree ceremonies may cause damage to the pages of an often very old lodge heirloom, and several lodges avoid this practice. However, other lodges adopt Genesis in the first degree for removing the blindfold, I Kings for the dimensions of King Solomon's temple in the second degree, and Ecclesiastes for the darker moments of the third degree, but many other options are traditionally used by different lodges.

First Business of the Lodge

Your first formal duty on a lodge night may be to process into the lodge room with the other Officers, in order to place the Principal Officers in their respective positions, and you will be carrying your sword of office. The sword may be carried vertically upwards or downwards within the lodge room, depending on the lodge traditions. It is normal that the Director of Ceremonies will precede you, so you follow him until you pause at each pedestal and turn inwards to allow that Principal Officer through to his seat. Having completed this, you will retire from the room and await communication from the Inner Guard. There are times when you can leave your post for a short time: to prepare candidates, to let brethren into the building if it is locked, etc., but there are other times when this is better avoided – the lack of prompt answering knocks from outside the lodge room usually causes temporary consternation within.

After the lodge has been formally opened the brethren may be asked to confirm who is staying to the festive board. The message from the Inner Guard may be something like 'Tyler's book less three', which hopefully takes into account those brethren who have not signed in and those not able to stay for the meal, but which will not mean a great deal to whoever is preparing the meal for the evening. You therefore have to translate this to numbers for the caterers, and remember that if you have an initiation during the evening the candidate will not be in the lodge room to indicate his presence, nor will he have signed the Tyler's book. Most Directors of Ceremonies remember this and add the words 'plus the candidate', but put it on your checklist anyway.

Latecomers and Visitors
About this time some latecomers may arrive, either lodge members or visitors that have been held up by traffic, work or whatever. They will need to be announced to the Inner Guard, and hopefully your lodge has slips of paper or cards that can be filled in by visitors to be handed to the Inner Guard and thence to the Secretary to record their attendance – your own lodge members you should begin to recognise. As a junior you may be perplexed by the hieroglyphics that are appended to some visitors' names, depicting either Provincial or Grand Lodge rank. Remember that many are the

equivalent to your own lodge Officers, although there are some additional ones to cause complications, but the visitors should be good-humoured enough to guide you through the various sets of initials – and perhaps their almost illegible handwriting, although as a junior you should perhaps be careful not to comment to this effect. And when announcing his presence, speak clearly so those people near the door of the lodge can hear you as well as the Inner Guard, and give the visitor's name and rank.

All visitors should be vouched for by a member of your lodge. Should a latecomer announce that he is not being so vouched for, because it is perhaps his first time in the lodge, then he will need to be proved. It is much preferable that he has made it on time and has already been assessed by the Director of Ceremonies and Junior Warden prior to the meeting, but this is not always possible. The Junior Warden is advised when he is appointed and invested that he is responsible for the examination of visitors, and in many lodges he will leave the lodge room to prove the visitor personally. If the Tyler is only a junior member of the lodge he will not be able to prove an Installed Master, for example, who wishes to attend the Inner Workings at an installation. This is one of the reasons why it may be preferable for a Past Master to occupy the office of Tyler; he is capable – if requested by the Junior Warden – of proving any visitor directly and reporting so to the Inner Guard when announcing that a brother seeks admission. It all makes for a smooth and efficient running of the lodge affairs, and the Junior Warden may have many other items of ritual on his mind for the meeting. Also note that the visitor only needs to be proved up to the highest degree that the lodge will be working in during the evening, and not necessarily to the full extent of his rank.

Preparation of Candidates

Your next duty may be the preparation of a candidate for the forthcoming ceremony. Note that candidates for the second and third degrees will exit the lodge after their question and answer session, and the preparation time you will have is relatively short; you have a little more time at your disposal with an initiate. Your role now is one of calming and reassuring the candidate. He may be nervous about what is to come or from the questions he was asked, and you can talk him through why you are preparing him the way you are, as well as 'we've all been through this', 'concentrate on the prompts from the Deacon', etc. In this sense an older hand outside the lodge room door can have a beneficial effect, but if you are a junior then you may have undergone the same ceremony relatively recently so you can perhaps recall more vividly how you felt at the time.

The details of the preparations are usefully given in the ritual book and also in the answers that candidates give before going into the next higher degree, so you can check your memory against the ritual book. Remember you are facing the candidate rather than seeing your own reflection in a mirror, so ensure the correct items of clothing are adjusted. In this sense the third degree is easy, because it is the first and second degree preparations combined, i.e. everything! Some lodges have their own clothing for candidates to put on, and make sure any such items are comfortably worn by the candidate prior to entry into the lodge room. You may also encounter an initiate who has a ring on a finger that cannot be easily removed and, if you have a plaster or other material in your own case or in the lodge effects to cover it, so much the better. With the more modern trend for earrings, nose-rings/studs and tongue-studs, the covering up may be more complicated than first imagined, and probably tongue-studs can be catered for as are gold fillings in teeth – leave well alone. For candidates with false limbs or wheelchairs, the Director of Ceremonies should have advised you what is expected.

You are then about to announce the candidate to the Inner Guard. Remember to give the correct knocks for initiation; some lodges use three and others only one, and a few lodges use three plus one. One of the older variations is for the three knocks to be louder and slower than normal, with reference being made to the number of knocks later in the ceremony. The same caveat applies in the other degrees when the candidate is returning to the lodge room for a higher degree to be conferred; you will normally be required to give the knocks appropriate to the candidate's current status, not those for the degree to which the lodge has been opened in preparation for the ceremony. In some lodges every candidate is always announced by one knock only, which saves any complications, but you should preserve your lodge's traditions where possible.

If you can learn the appropriate words, they will stand you in good stead when you are in a higher office (the Inner Guard and Deacons virtually repeat your words later in the ceremony), but if there is any uncertainty then use the ritual book – very few inside the lodge room will notice anything except an impeccable delivery. In fact the very start of the ceremony can affect how the whole event progresses; your hesitancy to the Inner Guard can affect his later delivery of the communication, and this often infects every member involved in performing the ceremony. By contrast, a smooth set of replies exactly as expected has a calming effect, and everything flows together exactly as it did at the perfect practice the lodge undoubtedly enjoyed a few days earlier.

Also remember that the candidate is required to reply to the questions of the Inner Guard, and you need to be next to him to prompt him if necessary, and this includes ensuring the correct pass grip required to re-enter the lodge is given. Until the candidate is formally inducted back into the lodge room, he is under your jurisdiction and, if there is any doubt in your mind about his physical preparation for the imminent ceremony, ensure the Inner Guard checks your handiwork.

After the practical part of the ceremony the candidate exits from the lodge room to adjust his mode of dress to a more normal state.

Again there may be a need for calming and reassurance, although most will be aware that the 'worst' is over. The candidate should be capable of attending to his own appearance, but you will need to ensure he is confident about the salutes he will be expected to give on his re-entry into the lodge room. I recall once when, as Tyler, I was assisting a new Master Mason to go through those signs, that the Inner Guard questioned what was taking the time and the lodge Organist began playing the funeral march – message understood! However, we practised a couple of times more, and then he went back into the lodge room. He performed the signs perfectly, which was alluded to with congratulations from several of the visitors that night, so the extra practice was well worthwhile, and after all your main job is to cater for the needs of the candidate whilst he is under your jurisdiction.

Other Lodge Business

If there is a lecture being delivered at the lodge meeting, you may be invited into the lodge room to hear it; the lodge is then 'tyled from within'. Remember to salute the Master on entering and before departing, unless your lodge permits the Tyler to slide in and out inconspicuously – note you are always expected to maintain the traditions of your lodge, even if they may appear to be slightly at variance with the standard ritual book.

Just before the end of the meeting you may have some senior Masons leaving the lodge room in advance of the others. They will normally be preceded by the lodge Deacons or Provincial Deacons in a formal procession, and the Inner Guard should inform you as he rises to prepare to open the door. If the Tyler assists the Inner Guard, perhaps because there are two doors, remember that the doors should be fully opened only after the first departing brother has saluted the Master, not before, and remember to be holding your sword at the carry (hand level with the waist, blade vertically upwards) as the brethren exit. While on the subject of opening the lodge room door, if there is ever an emergency such as a fire in the building, the normal lodge protocol should be dispensed with, the door opened and the cause of the interruption announced immediately. If the door is locked from within, then use three very loud knocks to summon the Inner Guard post haste.

As the meeting formally closes you may be expected to join in the procession escorting the Principal Officers out of the lodge room, especially if you have formally processed in at the start of the meeting. You may stand inside or outside the lodge room door as a guard of honour for the brethren to pass between, but you will doubtless be advised of this and you will probably have taken particular note of what the Tyler does ceremonially soon after you agreed to accept the Office for the coming year. All that remains now is to assist in tidying up the lodge room and ensuring that all of your lodge furniture is stored safely away.

You can now enjoy the remainder of the evening and the meal in particular, unless the Stewards are short-handed and you are asked to assist. Your final act is to give the Tyler's toast at the end of the festive board, which you will perform from the usual place in the room – perhaps facing the Master, behind his shoulder, etc. This will normally be a short version, but be aware that there are longer versions which may be used at installations or on other special evenings. If this is the case you will have been warned, or someone else will have been deputed or volunteered to deliver this toast on these special occasions.

Installations

We have already seen that senior brethren may leave the lodge room before the closing on a normal lodge night. If it is an installation meeting or another special occasion, the lodge may have some very senior Provincial Officers or even Grand Lodge Officers attending as formal representatives. If so, they will normally enter the lodge room in the first or third degree, but on these occasions you do not have to memorise all of the names and ranks – this duty usefully falls on the lodge Director of Ceremonies or his Provincial equivalent. You only have to ensure the doorway is fully open and you are standing with your sword at the carry for this formal entrance.

If the meeting is your lodge installation and you are moving out of office, then you will be carrying out your duties for the last occasion for some time. If yours is a lodge that uses an extended version of the Inner Workings, then as a junior (a Mason unqualified to be in a board of Installed Masters) you will have to be replaced by a Past Master like the Inner Guard, in which case you can enjoy your last few minutes as erstwhile Tyler of the lodge comfortably seated in the lodge room. Apart from the entrance and departure of the dignitaries, you may also have juniors leaving because the lodge is moving into a higher degree than they can attend, and obviously all those who are not Masters or Past Masters will have to leave for the Inner Workings. Some lodges delegate a senior member to accompany the juniors whenever they are evicted from the lodge room, so that they are not left alone twiddling their thumbs for what may seem a long time; otherwise you as Tyler can look after them during this part of the installation and also during the other degree ceremonies they have not yet undergone themselves. For the installation some lodges lay on refreshments for juniors during the Inner Workings, and indeed several lodges call off after the installation so that all attendees can partake of some refreshment – each has its own traditions.

Another item to check is that no junior Officers have left the lodge room still wearing their collars of office. If the lodge calls off during an installation, then it will be easy to insert the missing collars in their correct order in the interim, otherwise slide them in to the Inner Guard who will ensure they reach their correct destination in time. There should also have been prior agreement with the Director of Ceremonies about your own collar, because you will not have been in the lodge room to hand in your collar along with the other Officers of the lodge. You may have been asked not to wear it for this meeting, or you may hand it through the door of the lodge to the Inner Guard for him to hand in on your behalf, or you may surrender it when the lodge is called off. You might also check your Tyler's book to see if any Officers are absent, in which case their unused collars will also need to be taken from the anteroom into the lodge room in order to be re-invested onto new shoulders.

For the re-entry of juniors after the Inner Workings, it is normal to allow all visiting Master Masons to be re-seated – sometimes without saluting the new Master – in the third degree, and then to allow some or all of your own Master Masons to return. If the lodge has very few juniors, then it is probable that all will be admitted, but if a lodge is blessed with many juniors then you may send in roughly one-third each time the lodge progressively closes down through the three degrees. Note that Fellowcrafts and Entered Apprentices can obviously only be re-admitted into those degrees respectively and, if your lodge indulges in singing during the perambulations by the juniors, they will need copies of the appropriate words from you before they re-enter.

And then comes your own return into the lodge room at the end of your term as Tyler, if you have not already been replaced. If you are going up to Inner Guard this will be before the Stewards are appointed and invested, and someone will leave the lodge room to take your place outside the door with or without your sword until the next Tyler is invested and leaves the lodge room to take up his post. Remember to salute the new Master, and you will then be escorted to the East to receive your new Officer's collar. If you are moving up to Inner Guard your first duty may be to admit the Tyler's sword and collar if they are not already in the lodge room, and possibly you or another brother will temporarily step outside the door until the new Tyler arrives to take up his duties.

Hopefully you have had an interesting and varied year in office, and you are now prepared for further duties inside the lodge room. Remember that in future you cannot fall back on the ritual book – you need to know the words and actions fully this time, so perhaps outside the door of the lodge you have been following the ceremonies ready for your next role.

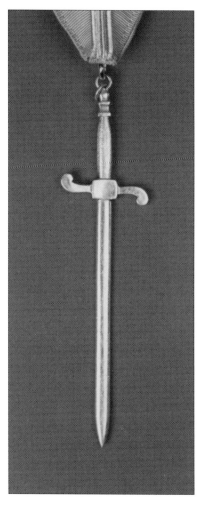

The Tyler's jewel which is a sword.

The Inner Guard

T his is the first office with specified ritual duties inside the lodge room, with the requirement that you need to know your role off by heart. On most occasions you will have interchanges with the Junior Warden, although sometimes you will address or be addressed by the Master directly. It will be useful if you know in which direction to make each communication, instead of provoking urgent hand signals around the lodge room to try to correct you.

Some Background to the Office

You are carrying out one of the sets of duties originally undertaken by the Junior Warden of the lodge. In some early lodges both Wardens were seated at the opposite end of the lodge room from the Master, and brethren entered between them; in other lodge rooms the Wardens were separated but the Junior Warden would attend to the door. Around the same time that the other Principal Officers had each gained an assistant in the form of the Deacons, probably from the Antient Grand Lodge which had a strong affinity with the workings of the lodges in Ireland, the Inner Guard appeared on lodge lists. The title of the office is fairly self-explanatory, and the link with the Tyler was emphasised in some of the early lodges by their adoption of the title Inner Tyler. The title Inner Guard came into being at the end of the 18th Century, and was included in the United Grand Lodge listing of lodge Officers from 1814 onwards.

In some lodges the Inner Guard was paid like the Tyler for each lodge night, and in the original Honour and Friendship lodge in Blandford (erased 1838) each new initiate received a shilling for taking on that office and assisting the Tyler in the meetings.

However, you will have heard at installations that the Junior Warden had the responsibility for proving visitors, and in the early lodges he would personally go to the door to check who wished to gain entry to the lodge room. If he recognised a lodge member or a regular visitor, the admission could be without delay, but if it were a stranger outside then he would retire from the lodge in order to satisfy himself that the brother could be admitted. The words 'warden' and 'guard' have much the same meaning with respect to protection or keeping, and several parallels are seen elsewhere. Churchwardens are essentially guardians of the church, a ward of court is placed under the protection of a guardian, a warden of regalia is the custodian or keeper of the items, to be 'on guard' is to be ready to protect yourself, while you may take certain actions to 'ward off' or protect yourself from evil. The interchangeability of the 'w' and 'gu' probably derives from our language being infected by the Norse and French invaders at different periods of our history, as seen in the English 'William' and the French 'Guillaume', for example.

The change from 'warden' to 'guard' to describe the person immediately in charge of the lodge room door is therefore not a major one, and it is probable when this Assistant Officer became an accepted appointment that it was decided to keep the title 'warden' for the Principal Officers, as well as perhaps also reflecting the door Officer's close working relationship with the Outer Guard or Tyler.

An Outline of the Duties
Your duties are briefly explained to you when you are formally appointed and invested at the installation. These include reporting to the Master when brethren claim admission, admitting Masons

on proof, receiving candidates in due form, and obeying the commands of the Junior Warden. Your jewel of office is two swords in saltire, i.e. crossed. The other Officers with crossed items on their jewels are the Director of Ceremonies and his Assistant with crossed wands, and the Secretary and his Assistant with crossed pens. In your case it probably symbolises that anyone who is admitted into the lodge room has run the gauntlet of two weapons: the Tyler's sword and your short dagger or poignard (another influence of the French in our past). In some of the early lodges, which did not approve of weapons being inside the lodge, the implement given to the Inner Guard was the trowel, although the larger pointed builders' trowels can become effective weapons if used as such. The only preparation that you will need for the ceremonies is to ensure that you always have your poignard at the door, and the large square and compasses for the second and third degree ceremonies respectively.

Before leaving your investiture as Inner Guard, a methodology for being escorted to and from the Master can be summarised as follows: stand when you are named by the Master; give your escort – probably the Director of Ceremonies, a court bow and proffer your right hand; walk in step with your escort to the Master; salute him before and/or after being invested as is your lodge custom; doubtless he will thank you for taking on the office, and you can briefly express your pleasure in accepting; walk escorted to the door of the lodge; receive the poignard offered you by the installing Inner Guard, handle towards you and resting on the left forearm; court bow to the installing Inner Guard and the Director of Ceremonies; and take your seat in the lodge. The general style is worth noting for all investitures, and remember the method of offering the poignard, because you will need to do the same to anyone replacing you at the door of the lodge, such as in the next installation, or when and if you bring the poignard to the Master during a first degree ceremony.

First Business of the Lodge

Your first formal duty of the evening may be to process into the lodge room in order to place the Principal Officers in their respective positions. Whether you process in or not, nothing will happen at the start of the lodge meeting until you close and/or lock the door, which signifies that the room is secure for the lodge to be opened. The Junior Warden will then ask you to see the lodge is properly tyled and you will open the door or the flap in the door or knock before replying, whichever is your lodge custom, but you will not salute – the lodge is not yet open. As this ceremony proceeds the Wardens assist the Master to open the lodge, and may

Inner Guard's seat emblem, Cambridge Masonic Hall — it is unusual to find that a special seat is created for the Inner Guard.

34

answer all of his questions directly. In other lodges the Officers are questioned directly by the Master. The Junior Warden will always reply on behalf of the Tyler, who is outside the lodge room, but be ready with your answers as the first Assistant Officer to be so addressed. As with the Tyler introducing candidates, if the first communications go smoothly then the whole ceremony seems to flow along, but if you are hesitant it often becomes infectious with the other Officers. If you are addressed by the Master or by the Junior Warden when the lodge is open you will need to salute, and you may do this with the poignard in the moving hand or not, depending on what your lodge prefers. Remember to speak audibly and clearly; the rushed and garbled response is never flattering to the Officer or the lodge. At the end of each opening ceremony you follow the Junior Warden and deliver the necessary knocks onto the lodge room door for the Tyler to reply to. One problem that could occur here is that he may be temporarily absent or slow to respond (he never falls asleep at his post – we hope!); you can peer through the communicating flap if there is one, or even open the door to see where he is, because the evening is unlikely to continue much further until the answering knocks are heard.

Latecomers and Visitors
Then just as you are about to settle down to enjoy the meeting you will have to cope with the first of sometimes frequent interruptions, these normally being latecomers. You will be advised not to leap straight out of your chair and start addressing the Junior Warden but, if there is no frantic urgency, to wait until the current part of the meeting or ceremony has been completed. The Secretary will prefer to finish his minutes in one session, and the Master will certainly not take kindly to being disturbed in the middle of an obligation. You should therefore arrange how the Tyler can quietly attract your attention, and no-one minds the Inner Guard rising to his feet and communicating with his colleague outside in low tones through the

flap in the door (but not through an open door), and then you can indicate to him when would be an appropriate moment to knock loudly on the door for your formal attention.

If it is a lodge member or a visitor, you will normally interact initially with the Junior Warden, who will often tell you to see who wants/seeks admission. This is equivalent to the format for allowing a candidate to enter the lodge, although the Emulation ritual strictly requires no response from the Junior Warden, which seems somewhat offhand and slightly rude. In some lodges you will continue the interaction with him in order to announce who is outside, and in other lodges you will address the Master directly – be aware of what your lodge expects. Hopefully the Tyler can hand you a visitor slip to read from, but there is usually a form of words that the lodge prefers to hear from the Inner Guard and it is not in the ritual books – you may need to indicate whose visitor he is, for example. Adopt the traditional procedure and wording, otherwise the person listening to your words may be temporarily confused by the unusual form of your announcement. And speak clearly so that everyone in the lodge, as well as the Junior Warden, can hear you and hold the sign until he has asked you to take the appropriate action, sometimes after repeating the message to the Master if required. In many cases the Director of Ceremonies or his Assistant or even a Deacon will come over to escort the brother formally, especially if he is of exalted rank or someone from overseas for example, but in some lodges the brother will make his own way into the lodge room. Either way, it is a courtesy to quietly remind him of which degree you are currently in, so that he does not make the wrong signs, although sometimes even this fails – you can only try.

In some lodges, prior to the induction of an initiate, the Treasurer and Secretary of the lodge will request permission to leave the lodge to attend to the candidate. This is usually to have him sign the required documents and relieve him of the necessary monies, which is a quick and fairly painless operation so that their absence is short and they will then need announcing and re-admitting.

Before the candidate re-enters the lodge for a second or third degree ceremony, the lodge will have to be opened into that higher degree. You have a short interchange with the Junior Warden to check that the lodge is tyled, either by looking or knocking, and then in some rituals you are supposed to follow the Junior Warden's opening knocks by tapping the sleeve of your left arm. This is to prevent the candidate from learning the knocks of a higher degree before he is yet qualified to do so, although it is unlikely that he would place much importance on the slightly different timing of the knocks, if indeed he noticed. The difficulty with this silent running procedure is that technically the Tyler does not know you are now in a higher degree, although fortunately he only uses the knocks of the lower degree to re-introduce the candidate. Surely it is more important for the Tyler to know what is happening in the lodge at all times; he may occasionally, before the candidate is admitted need to announce a latecomer into the lodge who should be able to hear the correct knocks as a check into which degree he is arriving. However, regardless of such considerations, you should always ensure that the format you use maintains your lodge traditions.

Admission of Candidates
The person other than a visitor who may be seeking admission is an initiate or a candidate for a higher degree. For the latter he will have already been escorted to the door by a Deacon after entrusting, so you are aware of who will be returning. A word of warning when the Tyler knocks to announce a candidate is coming to be passed or raised. He will usually give the knocks appropriate to the candidate's current status and not for the degree to which he seeks to be admitted. You on the other hand are inside the lodge room, and you will normally be expected to give the sign of the degree in which the lodge is now operating, so do not be fooled by the knocks

and assume you should make the equivalent sign. It is something that members and visitors will be keeping an eye out for, because they know you are a junior, to see if you have taken on board the significance of the communications through the door. Your first gentle reminder may be the Junior Warden using the correct sign, and you then wishing the floor would open up to receive you!

Whilst you are interacting with the Tyler, check that the candidate has been properly prepared by him. You immediately have to inform the Master that the candidate is ready for entry into the lodge, and it does not look very professional if the Director of Ceremonies has to come over to change an item of the candidate's attire before proceeding with the ceremony. In the second and third degree ensure the candidate knows the password, as again you volunteer to the Master that he does, but allow the Tyler to adjust the pass grip if the candidate is unsure. You then let the candidate into the lodge when the Deacons arrive, and at the same time raise the appropriate implement high so that the Master and the lodge can see that you have applied it.

For all candidates there is a set form of words, used by first the Tyler and you, and then by you and the Master. Usefully the second communication is virtually identical to what the Tyler tells you, so you will have received a very recent reminder of the correct phrases before you have to restate them. Note that some lodges prefer to adopt the word 'alarm' when a candidate is to be admitted, but many seem to accept the word 'report' from the Inner Guard. You then wait for the Deacon or Deacons to come to the door to escort the candidate in before opening the door, and again until the door is re-secured there should be no words spoken or actions undertaken inside the lodge room.

In a first degree ceremony you may be required to pass the poignard up to the East, where it will be alluded to later in the ceremony, but each lodge has its own route for this to happen – carried by the Senior Deacon, or passed hand to hand by the brethren sitting along the North side of the lodge room, or whatever. In some lodges the Inner Guard walks to the Master and proffers him the poignard, handle first and on the left forearm, when he wants to explain to the candidate what he felt at his first entrance into the lodge. You then walk smartly back to the door while the Master moves on to the cable tow.

In a higher degree ceremony you may be in charge of the lodge room lighting and will have to make the appropriate adjustments at the required time, but you should have been briefed on this and practised it beforehand.

Other Lodge Business
You can now settle down and enjoy the ceremony or lecture, safe in the knowledge that only when one or both Deacons approach you again with the candidate after he has saluted the Master will you need to open the door again. Very occasionally someone may ask permission to leave the room for a while, and he may arrive unescorted, and he will then require his return to be announced, unless traditionally your lodge allows him back in without undue fuss. A candidate returning will have to be formally announced to the Junior Warden and a Deacon will come to collect him, so again you only open the door when the Deacon is in position at the door. By this time even the latecomers will have given up coming, so there should be no further disturbances from outside the lodge. In some lodges some or all of the Stewards retire early to prepare the festive board, and the senior Masons present may elect to leave before the closing ceremony, and you may have the additional unenviable task of holding a collection plate for them to use if your lodge takes its charity collections during the closing ode or hymn.

The only other item to cause you any concern is if there are no answering knocks from the Tyler on the door of the lodge room when opening or closing a degree. After a reasonable pause to enable him to skip across the anteroom, you should open the door to check where he is – even step outside very briefly and call for him. The Tyler may be handing in the meal bookings, or preparing the candidate in an adjoining room, so do not necessarily think the worse of him being asleep or propping up the bar. If, however, he is nowhere to be found, you should report to the Junior Warden, and a substitute will be sent outside the room until the Tyler returns – the lodge must be guarded outside at all times that it is in session.

For certain lectures or other lodge business the lodge is called off and back on again. This is the one time you do not repeat the Junior Warden's knocks to the Tyler – the first he knows that the lodge has changed modus operandi is when the door opens and people file out or he is invited into the room. In any case your agreed bush telegraph system of communication should have forewarned him that this was about to happen; it is courtesy to keep your co-worker as fully informed as possible of what is happening in the lodge. If your lodge calls off during an installation then this will not be your problem, as the installing Inner Guard will have replaced you before then.

You will have a final interaction with the Junior Warden during the closing, and this time you will salute because the lodge is open. Then there is a final set of knocks on the door to inform the Tyler it is all over – and to warn him to be ready to process into the lodge to escort the Principal Officers out at the end of the meeting if that is the way your lodge does it. You have now finished for the evening, unless the lodge is short of Stewards, with not even a toast to propose at the festive board like the Tyler, so congratulate the candidate if there has been a degree ceremony and also those who have worked so hard in the lodge room, and enjoy the festive board.

Installations

At the installation you may be involved in opening up to the third degree, and you will doubtless have to induct a mini-procession of dignitaries who have come as the representative of the Provincial or District Grand Master and his escort. Apart from opening the door at the appropriate time, the only unusual item you will probably announce is the return of the lodge Director of Ceremonies, or his Provincial equivalent seeking admission – the complications of names and titles engendered by having senior visitors attending are thankfully theirs to cope with. If your office collars are formally handed in, it will often be juniors first so that the order in which the collars are deposited is the reverse of the order in which they will be invested on the new Officers. This is perhaps the only time you will be expected to leave your post at the door, and even then in some lodges a colleague will take the collar up for you so that you can stay where you are.

If you are a junior Mason, i.e. you have not yet attained the office of Master, you will need to be replaced by a Past Master along with the Wardens; all juniors have to leave so that the Inner Workings are restricted to those entitled to be there. You will then leave the

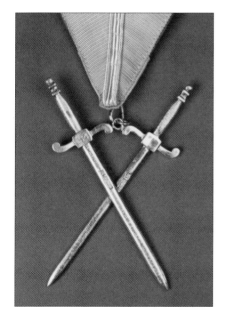

lodge room when requested to do so, enjoy the refreshments that the lodge has hopefully laid on for you, and afterwards be ready to return to the lodge to salute the new Master and for the appointment of his Officers. If the Inner Guard is already a Past Master he may be requested to stay in post, and he will have to allow the juniors to retire and return at the

Inner Guard's jewel of Lodge of Peace & Unity No 314, Preston.

41

appropriate junctures of the proceedings as requested by the Installing Master.

During your term as Inner Guard as a junior you have doubtless been keenly watching the Deacons going through their paces, so that you are fully prepared for your next step towards the Chair of the lodge. The year as Inner Guard is a relatively quiet one and is a time when you can study in closer detail the operation of the lodge and the roles of the different Officers, but it is probably the office which copes with the most interruptions as brethren come and go – either as decreed in the ceremonies or unexpectedly, so from time to time you could have been kept on your toes.

The Deacons

Having enjoyed one or two years at the door of the lodge, either with the book outside or permanently rooted at the door on the inside, you are now entering the choreography of the ceremonial – you have to move around the lodge room. Not only that, but you also have to escort a candidate who may not have a clue what you are doing or where you are going, and who may not repeat exactly what you instruct him to say, so this is definitely a major step up in responsibility. In fact the success of the ceremonies very much depends on how good you are; the other lodge members can be word-perfect, but if the candidate is in the wrong place at the wrong time it is no longer impressive.

You are one of a pair, just like the Wardens, and in many ways you work as a sub-team as do the Tyler and Inner Guard together. It looks infinitely better when both of you are processing around the lodge in the same style; if one of the Deacons carries his wand vertically and the other leans his wand on his shoulder, the image of operating as a team becomes somewhat distorted. As the Senior Deacon has normally already been inducted into the lodge traditions when he was the Junior Deacon, it is perhaps sensible for him to school his new colleague in those same traditions, although in all probability the Director of Ceremonies will also give both Deacons some advice on how he wants them to work together. If the Deacons are of exactly the same stature then one mirroring the other will be easy to achieve, but if they are of significantly different heights for example, then some adjustments to style may be necessary to create the desired effect in various situations.

This is a time when it can be categorically said that 'practice makes perfect', and the lodge and the Director of Ceremonies and his Assistant will do their utmost to ensure you are brimming with confidence about your new responsibilities. Having now frightened the life out of you with this build-up, it is really not all that onerous and, once you have mastered the basic choreography of the various perambulations, the ceremonies are deceptively easy to follow.

Some Background to the Office

The Deacons did not figure in the very early English lodges, but neither did the other junior Officers except the Tyler. Sometimes it would be the candidate's proposer or seconder who would guide him round the lodge room, or the Junior Warden could do so if these two were not able to be present.

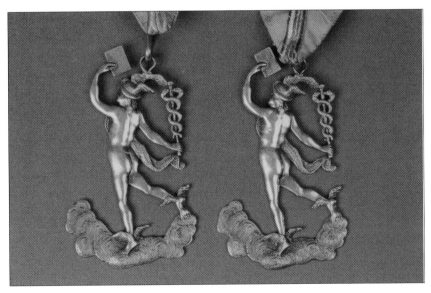

Deacons' Mercury jewels of the Lodge of Peace & Unity No 314, both carrying the minute book?

The word Deacon is derived from the Greek *diakonos* and the Latin *diaconus*, meaning servant, waiting-man, helper or messenger. They were referred to in the New Testament as having leading roles in the organisation in the churches, and still have their place in modern churches. In the Anglican Church the ministry enfolds the Bishop, Priest and Deacon in order of precedence; in the Roman Catholic Church the Deacon assists the priest in various duties.

Deacons were appointed early on in some of the Moderns' lodges, the Moderns' or Premier Grand Lodge having been established in 1717, and from 1727 onwards some lodges were minuting the appointment of Deacons. Grand Lodge itself did not appoint Deacons, but some of its lodges must have been following older traditions or were influenced by Irish Freemasonry. Sometimes they were referred to as 'Senior Deacon or Steward' followed by a 'Deputy Steward', so some lodges may have been placing the Deacons at the top of the Stewards' list. In other lodges the terms 'Master's Deacon' and 'Warden's Deacon' were adopted, and occasionally after the name Deacon had been introduced the title of the office appears to have later reverted back to Steward.

After the Antient Grand Lodge was formed in 1751, being largely based on Irish Freemasonry where Deacons were regularly appointed, almost all of the Antient lodges had Deacons. Many military lodges, warranted to meet where they could rather than in a fixed meeting place, were of Antient or Irish descent, and with their acceptance of the hierarchy of command, they would be used to junior officers carrying messages to and from their seniors. This messenger aspect of the work is also recorded in some non-military lodges, where two Entered Apprentices had white rods, the senior being placed in the North to carry messages from the Master to the Senior Warden. The junior was to stand at the inside of the door to welcome brethren and convey messages to the Tyler, as a joint Junior Deacon and Inner Guard, so the separation into the two current positions must have occurred somewhat later. Interestingly in many American lodges there is no Inner Guard, but the door of the lodge is guarded by the Junior Deacon, whilst the Senior Deacon alone conducts the candidates through the three degrees.

When the two Grand English Lodges began discussions on amalgamating, they set up a Special Lodge of Promulgation to ascertain the ancient landmarks of the Order in 1809, and within one month it had been agreed that Deacons were 'not only Ancient but useful and necessary Officers' in a lodge. With this decision, several more Moderns' lodges began appointing Deacons, and they were evident in United Grand Lodge from 1814 onwards, and in all private lodges shortly thereafter.

Nowadays the jewel of the Deacon is a dove bearing an olive branch, but this has only been the norm in England since the creation of United Grand Lodge. The Antient lodges, following the style of some Irish lodges, tended to adopt this recognised symbol of peace as well as messenger (the trees were coming into leaf after the Great Flood). Some Antient lodges had adopted a winged Mercury (Roman) or Hermes (Greek) messenger of the Gods, and several of the older lodges retain these jewels today. The Moderns' lodges, some of whom had appointed Deacons before 1751, had not always designated a jewel for them. In later years, before the Union, those lodges who appointed Deacons to office also sometimes used a Mercury figure, whilst a few lodges in the North East of the country adopted a radiant sun and a crescent moon.

With these latter lodges it is not always known for which Principal Officer the Deacon was operating; the moon is associated with the Senior Warden, but the sun is associated in the opening of the lodge with all the three Principal Officers. In the first degree ceremony, however, the lesser lights are introduced to the candidate as the Junior Warden representing the sun and the Senior Warden representing the moon. Furthermore, in some older lodges the Deacons sat next to the Wardens and were expected to deputise for them, in which case the sun presumably designated the Junior

Deacon, as the Senior Warden represented the moon. In those other lodges that had a Master's Deacon and a Senior Warden's Deacon, the sun would be associated with the former and the moon with the latter. United Grand Lodge obviously decided on the arrangement with a Deacon attributed to the Master, but perhaps avoided the issue of which jewel for each Officer by adopting the doves – and in the context of there having been an agreeable and peaceable Union of the two Grand Lodges, this may also have been seen as a symbolic gesture.

The duties of the Deacons have been developed and modified over the years, and nowadays they perform many of those original duties, except attending to the door of the lodge is currently left to the Inner Guard, but conducting the candidates through the ceremonies is seen by many as now the most important aspect of their work.

The Degree Ceremonies

As a Deacon you now have a special duty in the lodge – to escort the candidates around the lodge room. The three ceremonies are variations on a theme, and for the temporarily unthinking it is relatively easy to transpose from one into another. In order to remember exactly what you need to do in each and when, it is worthwhile breaking down the format into its constituent parts. The initiation begins differently from the other degrees, because a non-Mason is being inducted for the first time, but the basic parts of the ceremonies all fall into four distinct elements: the presentation, obligation, demonstration and explanation, which are amplified as follows:

PRESENTATION (differs between the first and the other degrees)

First degree:
Introduction – the candidate enters the lodge and kneels for prayer.

Presentation – the Master announces that the candidate is making a circuit of the lodge in order to be introduced formally to the Wardens, after which the Senior Warden presents the candidate to the Master.

Second and third degrees:
Introduction – the Master introduces and tests the candidate verbally on the knowledge he gained from the previous degree ceremony.

Entrusting (test of merit) – the candidate is given the pass grip and password in order to re-enter the lodge in a higher degree, and he retires to be prepared physically.

Presentation – the candidate re-enters and makes one or two circuits of the lodge, communicating the signs, tokens and words of the first degree (to the Junior Warden) and second degree (to the Senior Warden) as appropriate. The Master then announces that the candidate is making his final circuit of the lodge, in order to communicate the test of merit to the Senior Warden, after which the latter presents the candidate to the Master.

Standard to all degrees:

OBLIGATION
Obligation – the Deacon guides the candidate correctly to the East, who then takes and seals his obligation, and the position of the square and compasses is explained; in the third degree there is an additional extensive section on the symbolism of death.

Entrusting (signs) – the candidate is shown the signs, tokens and words, the last two being repeated with the Deacon (except in the third degree), and the penalties are also explained.

DEMONSTRATION
Demonstration – the candidate is presented to the Wardens to practise and display his new information (not in the third degree).

Investiture – of the new apron, usually by the Senior Warden; followed by appropriate remarks on what the new role entails, including a major description of charity in the first degree.

EXPLANATION
Working Tools – their symbolism is explained (follows the traditional history in the third degree).
Charge – although the first degree charge is always delivered, the charges after the other ceremonies are delivered less frequently.
Tracing Board – the second and third degree tracing boards are usually delivered in the ceremony (the third is in the traditional history) rather than the charge, whilst in the first degree the tracing board, which contains a wealth of information of great interest to a newcomer, is more rarely delivered.
Questions and Answers – in some lodges at the end of the first or second degree, the candidate is shown a rehearsal of the answers he will need to learn before presenting himself for the next degree.

It can be seen that the second and third degrees add an entrusting between the introduction and the presentation, and an entrusting is almost always followed by a demonstration of previous and/or new knowledge, as is also seen after the obligation. Whenever a candidate is kneeling for prayer or for an obligation, the Deacons will always cross their wands over his head, held in their left hands, and adopt the appropriate sign with their right hands.

The rule of thumb is that the total number of circuits made by the candidate equals the degree being conferred. In the first degree the Junior Deacon has only one circuit to do, and he waits for the Master's announcement before starting; the Senior Deacon has two circuits in total for a second degree and three for a third, and he too awaits the Master's announcement before starting the final lap. In many lodges both Deacons accompany the initiate throughout the first degree until he retires from the lodge – he is new to Freemasonry, and perhaps should not be left to stand alone at any time during the ceremony. In the second and third degree the candidate has more experience of Freemasonry, and the Senior Deacon often performs the escort duties alone, but there are variations on this theme in different lodges.

The main job of the Deacon is to ensure that the candidate is placed at the correct position for the next part of the ceremony. Up until the candidate being invested with his apron the format is common to almost all lodges, but the remaining items will vary from lodge to lodge, depending on how the lodge organises the delivery of those later items in the ceremony. When escorting the candidate around the lodge room, the Deacons come into direct contact with all of the Principal Officers as well as the Inner Guard, and in learning the interchanges with the former you are at the same time learning what you will be saying when you are holding those offices in the future.

There are the other aspects of lodge business that fall on the shoulders of the Deacons, such as the conducting of ballots, and this aspect is dealt with later. With regard to latecomers, members or visitors, in most lodges the Director of Ceremonies or his Assistant will attend to these entrances, so there is usually no involvement for the Deacons. If there are Entered Apprentices or Fellowcrafts who need to retire before a higher degree is conferred, then it is usual for the Junior Deacon to collect and escort the former out of and back into the lodge room, and for the Senior Deacon to look after the latter. This is a useful service to perform, as often these relatively new Masons are not totally sure of the correct protocol, and they appreciate the guidance the Deacons can give. In the installation meeting when those below an Installed Master need to leave the proceedings – and this will include the Deacons if they are juniors – it is usual for all of those retiring from the lodge room to salute from their places and to leave by the shortest route, and no escort is required.

The Junior Deacon

Your previous experience of work in the lodge room was standing up and sitting down as Inner Guard, and possibly being escorted as a junior or Steward to where you delivered part of the ceremony to a candidate or part of a lecture. You now have to make your own way around the lodge room, so you need to know where you are going. There is the bonus that you have a colleague who has just been through this office in the previous year, and for much of the time he can gently coach you through the various parts of your duties, but there are occasions when it is up to you alone.

One benefit of being Junior Deacon is that you are entrusted with guiding the candidate through only one of the ceremonies, whilst you merely assist your senior colleague in the two ceremonies for which he takes the lead. The downside of this splitting of responsibilities is that yours is the candidate who knows least about what to expect. Additionally he is blindfolded for the first part of the ceremony, so you will need to be vigilant in ensuring that he is guided carefully to the appropriate positions around the lodge room.

It is therefore useful for you to introduce yourself to the candidate, whether or not you have met him socially before, so that he can enter the lodge room with the confidence that someone he has met will be there to look after him throughout the whole ceremony. At the same time you can warn him there will be occasions when he is expected to speak for himself, and others when he should wait for your prompt, so that you have established a preliminary working relationship that enables him to relax and perhaps even enjoy the ceremony as it unfolds. And if his proposer or seconder has not yet done so, you can introduce the candidate to the other members of the lodge with whom he will be interacting during the meeting – without detracting from the solemnity of the occasion, let him know he is among friends.

An Outline of the Duties

Your duties are explained at your appointment and investiture during the installation meeting. They include carrying communications between the Senior and Junior Wardens, as well as attending on candidates being initiated and assisting in the other two ceremonies. After having been invested and conducted to your place in the lodge, you should give a court bow to your escort, sit, and place your wand in its holder, or vice versa if that is your lodge tradition. Your first actions at the meeting will be in the lodge closing and possibly escorting senior brethren and the Master out of the lodge room at the end of the evening. But it may be better to start at the opening of a lodge and run through all of the items in which you will be involved.

First Business of the Lodge

Your first job may be as part of the procession escorting the Master and Wardens into the lodge room at the start of the standard meeting. As well as facing inwards when each Principal Officer in turn is placed behind his pedestal, it may be the tradition in your lodge for the Deacons to cross their wands for the Officer to pass under. Already you need to have an understanding with the Senior Deacon how high up the wands you intend to make the cross – near the top or lower down; Deacons with wands at significantly different angles rarely look co-ordinated. You probably stay at the Senior Warden's pedestal once he is placed in position; as the junior you will be on the outermost column of Officers in the procession and so close to your seat in the lodge at this juncture, while the Senior Deacon accompanies the Director of Ceremonies as far as his place near to the Master.

During the formal opening of the lodge you may be required to answer the Master directly about your position in the lodge room and your duties, and you will be following the Inner Guard as the Master works his way up the list of Officers. Once the lodge has been declared open, in any degree, it is usual for the Deacons to ensure that the correct tracing board is displayed. If the boards are in the centre of the lodge room the Deacons work as a pair, especially if this involves turning boards over or sliding them out of a holder, but if the tracing boards are located at the pedestals of the Principal Officers or elsewhere, it is usual for the nearest Deacon to attend to it. To maintain the style with which this is done in your lodge – for example do you carry your wands or not? – it would have been useful to take note of the procedure when you were acting as Inner Guard, but the Senior Deacon or Director of Ceremonies can quickly put you right at a practice meeting. If for example the Junior Deacon attends to the tracing boards, working tools, Book of Constitutions, etc., and they are in the centre of the lodge room, you will hand your wand to your senior colleague while you arrange those items of lodge furniture as required. If the tracing boards are leaning against one pedestal in a single set, they will need to be rotated in turn, usually by holding first one then two then all three boards in the different degrees, so it is a manoeuvre worth practising and also worth checking that the boards are in the correct order at the start of the meeting. It should also be noted that it is not strictly necessary to hide the first degree board when exposing the second degree board if the boards are separate (it is unavoidable if they are stacked together as a set) as the lodge has not been formally closed in the first degree, but your lodge custom may dictate otherwise.

At the closing of any degree, the same procedure is followed with regard to the tracing boards but in reverse. If your lodge has a formal retiring procession after finally closing the lodge, you will be the first Officer to move if the Inner Guard and Tyler are not involved, and the procedure is likely to be a variation of the following. During the closing ode you will go to the Senior Deacon and move off as a pair to collect first the Junior and then the Senior Wardens. You then pass the Master's pedestal for the second time, without any salute as the lodge is closed, and halt in the South West of the lodge room, possibly behind the Assistant Director of Ceremonies, to wait for the procession to form up behind. You will precede the Master and his Wardens to the door at the command of the Director of Ceremonies, then turn inwards and cross wands for the procession to pass beneath them as it finally exits from the room, or whatever variation on this theme your lodge prescribes.

An additional option exercised by some lodges is that when the Immediate Past Master opens or closes the Book in the East, he will do so under the crossed wands of the Deacons. This means that the Junior Deacon has to make his way to the East to be joined by the Senior Deacon at the propitious moment, and you then return to your seat. One or both Deacons may also be delegated to attend to the lighting of the candles at the pedestals, which will hopefully mean that the lodge possesses a taper, cigarette lighter or a box of matches. Be wary of attempting the challenge of lighting all three with one match – this is fraught with dangers, not least of which may be that you could burn your fingers or gloves towards the end of your circuit! However, some lodges include the lighting of candles in their opening ritual, even in these days of electric lighting, as a way of formally igniting the lesser lights, and this may be perpetuating the traditions of the earlier lodges when candles and oil lamps were the only means of illumination.

After the opening of a lodge, the minutes of the previous meeting are either read out by the Secretary or, if already circulated to members beforehand, confirmed directly. In some lodges the Wardens as well as the Master countersign the minutes, and this is one of the few occasions you will carry out the first part of your duties as described at the installation. The Senior Deacon will bring the book to the Senior Warden to sign and will then hand it to you for you to carry it to the Junior Warden for signature. You may then be required to return the book to the Senior Deacon still waiting at the Senior Warden's pedestal and, once he has returned the book to the Secretary, the Deacons sit down together. It is a delightful sequence that takes very little extra time, and it is sometimes the only occasion when each Deacon actually processes between his pair of Principal Officers as he was told he would do when being appointed. Another point to note is that in their perambulations some lodges salute all of the Principal Officers, some only the Master, and they can do so in passing or by coming to a halt. The Deacons may be required to lean their wands against their shoulders before saluting, or they may still carry them in one or other hand, so again you need to be aware of how your lodge likes to see this courtesy performed.

Escorting Candidates

First Degree
Presentation
And now comes your big moment – you are asked to collect the initiate from the door. You will normally wait for the Senior Deacon to perambulate round to you and go as a pair to the door, with him peeling off to attend to the kneeling cushion or stool on the way. The Inner Guard steps aside and you take the candidate by the arm, and then you begin to realise how little he is able to assist you in moving anywhere. This is a time when at the previous practice meetings the substitute for the candidate, by acting apparently awkwardly, can have given you a real insight of what it

will be like on the night, so the preparation will stand you in good stead.

In fact, your preparation should have included meeting the candidate on the evening of the meeting. You can explain in general terms what you will be doing and what you will be requesting him to do and perhaps even the rough timescale of events. The candidate will feel much more confident in being directed by someone who has taken the time to make himself known, albeit for only a couple of minutes, so even this short exchange can greatly benefit your own labours during the evening. And is it not a courtesy that all of the lodge members, who will be involved with escorting and addressing the candidate during the ceremony, introduce themselves to him before the meeting starts?

The next actions are basically as detailed in the ritual book, the Master addressing the candidate and you prompting his answers, instructing him where to kneel and supporting his balance while he is doing so, another prompt and then the candidate regains his feet. Note that the candidate does not normally give any sign during the prayer, as he knows little if anything about the workings in lodge. You then wait for the Master to announce that the candidate will be taken round the lodge to be presented to the Wardens.

Having been so directed, you are now ready for the perambulation. This will be much more easily performed if you and the candidate can fall into step together, which hopefully you have warned him about, but if there is a major size difference between you and him, then you may have to adjust your steps to his. Whichever course you choose, do not appear to be hurried and your show of control and confidence will be communicated to him, and by taking your time it allows you to think through what aspects of the ceremony come next whilst on the move.

A word on how to hold the candidate: if you try to walk around holding hands loosely at hip height, he will have absolutely no idea where you are trying to direct him. You need a firm grip on his hand by grasping his palm or even by interlacing the fingers, and preferably with his arm tucked inside yours. In this way when you stop or turn, then a lot of his arm is tightly attached to you, and after one or two failed attempts by him to go off in some other direction he will quickly learn to follow your lead promptly. And do keep quietly warning him of every change in direction and movement, so that his body is ready for an alteration of course, and he should enter into the spirit of the occasion. When you lower your arm it is a signal that you want to release the grip, and again he will rapidly understand the warning of what is about to happen.

There are two presentations at the Wardens' pedestals, with the words almost identical to those you heard from the Inner Guard at the door of the lodge room. You will have to guide the candidate's hand to strike the Wardens, and you will do this from the front or the side of the pedestals, assisted by the Wardens leaning forward. No matter what you think of the Wardens, these actions are symbolic and should not be a bruising encounter. If you perform this action on the right-hand side of the Wardens' pedestals and the tracing boards are leaning against the pedestals, remember to back out far enough that you and your blindfolded candidate do not trip over them during the next part of the perambulation. You then wheel the candidate round for him to be formally presented by the Senior Warden to the Master, and you are ready to advance with the candidate to the East. It is worth noting that when the Senior Warden is presenting the candidate to the Master, the people lined up in the West of the lodge should be the Senior Warden, candidate, Junior Deacon and Senior Deacon, if the lodge room can accommodate four abreast.

Obligation and Demonstration

The Senior Warden directs you to escort the candidate to the East. In some lodges the Junior Deacon turns and salutes the Senior Warden when he is addressed, in others he merely remains stationary, but in your eagerness to start the tour of the lodge room do not move off too early – it makes it look as if an errant child is being pulled up. You take the candidate partway to the East, so that there is enough distance in which to make the final approach to the pedestal.

The three steps, whether announced formally as of different length or not, are difficult to judge exactly and few of the onlookers will mind a minor miscalculation. You may even be able to judge by the confidence or otherwise of your candidate what length of stride he will probably take, and adjust your initial placement accordingly. Some Deacons tell him to step forward until his foot hits the wand they have grounded in front of him, but many candidates are able to function without that mechanical aid. A final shuffle is not a disaster, and it is better that the candidate feels the kneeling stool in front of him, so that he is forewarned about the height he needs to be prepared for. Another method is to move the candidate's held hand forward by the distance you want him to step, and often the candidate will move forward enough to catch up his hand again. Your wand can also be used to persuade the candidate to place his feet at right angles, by gently tapping the side of the foot until it is in the correct position.

At the pedestal you follow the Master's instructions to the candidate, prompt any answers that are hesitated over, and help the Master by proffering the candidate's right hand to him. With regard to the candidate holding the implement in his left hand, often the Master and Senior Deacon will help him, and then you cross wands with your fellow Deacon. In some lodges the Director of Ceremonies joins in, and to some extent his wand serves to stabilise the others, but without this third wand you need to have agreed with your colleague at what height you are crossing otherwise it can appear lop-sided. Your wand will be in your left hand, because you will be standing to order for the obligation, and then you may have to discharge the sign early because you need to instruct the candidate how to seal his obligation. Some lodges discharge the sign after the obligation, some after its sealing, and the sign used may be that of the degree or of fidelity, depending on the preference of your lodge. Uncross the wands and gently persuade the candidate to lean forward by a slight pressure on the back of his head, whispering instructions to him if he seems uncertain what to do. Then hope that the Tyler has not created a knot that requires Alexander's solution for the Gordian Knot, a sword stroke; otherwise enjoy the benefits of modern fastenings such as Velcro on the blindfold. However, in most lodges after you have undone the fastening, you still hold the blindfold in place until the appropriate moment as conducted by the Master.

Afterwards the Master delivers a series of explanations, which once the candidate regains his feet will require a slight adjustment of positioning in order for him to see what is being pointed out, after which you need to place the candidate ready to have the dangers and penalties explained and to be taught the signs. In some lodges he faces East in front of the pedestal, in others he goes up alongside the North of the pedestal, and in yet others the Master comes onto the lodge room floor to conduct operations. You need to ensure that the candidate again follows the instructions given him, correcting his hand when necessary, and then prompting the answers he needs to give. You may have warned him that at this stage he waits for your prompt, even if it transpires that he has a very good short-term memory for what has gone before. You will have seen this routine many times in the lodge before, so you are merely trying to maintain the lodge traditions.

The ritual decrees that the word is either lettered or halved. In many lodges the Master first spells out the word so that the candidate understands what it is, and then when you are prompting the candidate to reply to the Master with caution you will halve the word. If you then letter the word with the Junior Warden and halve it with the Senior Warden, the candidate will have practised both methods. In some lodges the word is lettered and also halved in the same sequence before saying the entire word, which appears to contradict the preamble that you prompt the candidate to say beforehand.

If the Master has left his seat in order to communicate the secrets, wait with your candidate until he is reseated. You then make another perambulation to the Wardens to introduce the candidate, this time as a brother and allowing him, under your direction, to display his new-found knowledge. You ensure that the candidate uses the correct grip with the Wardens, and you must be careful not to let the candidate say the word, as you are teaching him to be cautious in communication, so either speak instantly after the Warden has asked for the word, or place a hand on the candidate's shoulder to warn him to wait until you have dictated the answer. In fact with the Senior Warden the sign is dissected into its component parts so that each can be explained, and again you need to ensure the candidate does not get ahead of himself. After the second set of exchanges, you wheel the candidate round in order to let the Senior Warden present him to the Master and then invest him with his first apron. This may involve some more minor shuffling so that the Senior Warden can operate comfortably at the side of his pedestal, and you can assist him by holding the apron strings behind the candidate whilst they are being tied off at the front.

Following this the Master makes a few additional observations, and then instructs you directly to place the candidate elsewhere in the lodge room. This is the first time you have deviated from a standard perambulation to the three pedestals, so know the geography of your lodge room, whether you show the candidate what to do or merely instruct him, and this may involve the rough ashlar if one is normally placed on the floor of the lodge. You then stand aside or to the rear of the candidate so that you can pick up a collection plate if appropriate. At the prescribed moment you face him to make the necessary enquiries, and then report to the Master and return to your former position. As when addressing the Wardens, do not try to rush the words; they are not many in number, and clarity far outweighs speed in this instance. It is useful for the candidate, who may be uncertain over exactly what answers are required, to have the Senior Deacon standing alongside; otherwise you can indicate the expected reply with a shake or a nod of your head as appropriate.

Explanation
The Master now instructs you to move the candidate elsewhere for the explanation of the working tools, and again you need to know exactly where they will be presented so that you do not appear to be wandering aimlessly round the lodge room. Some lodges insist on squaring everything, others allow movement directly to the desired destination, and you will know into which category your lodge falls.

   The warrant, book and by-laws are then presented, normally back in the East (and you need to return there usually without instruction), and then you escort the candidate so that he can retire from the lodge. Remember to instruct him to salute the Master before leaving, and this you may do with him or by instruction alone, depending on tradition; then wheel him around, usually keeping yourself between him and the Master, and hand him over to the Tyler. You can then return to your seat, hopefully to the plaudits of the members and visitors for a job well done.

   When the candidate returns, you hope that his sign on entry will be as immaculate as his revitalised appearance, and then you place him appropriately for the Charge. Normally you will be operating on your own, but in several lodges both Deacons are again involved. In some lodges other items can also be explained, such as the tracing board, the mode of preparation that the candidate underwent, and perhaps even a formal presentation of his gloves. You may be required to stand with the candidate throughout, or you may leave him to listen alone. Then finally you can escort him to a seat in the lodge room that he will be very relieved to settle into, normally in the North East, and you can return to your place in the West.

Second and Third Degrees

In these ceremonies it is the Senior Deacon who takes charge most of the time, although often it is the Junior Deacon who collects the Entered Apprentice who is going to be passed and positions him to answer the test questions, which may be in the centre of the lodge or in the North West. You hope that he can answer all of them with confidence, but you need to know the answers yourself in case he requires a prompt – it does not look dignified for the Director of Ceremonies or someone else having to volunteer the prompts. Try to prompt the candidate as quietly as possible, because he should be seen to be able to answer them as fully as possible himself, and in olden days he may well have had his next ceremony deferred until he had been confidently able to do so. These days some lodges seem to hurry their candidates through the three degrees as quickly as possible, but we are in effect re-enacting the apprentice demonstrating his proficiency in what he had to learn off by heart before being entrusted with the next level of information.

You then take the candidate to the Master for entrusting with the pass grip and password, and be prepared again to prompt the candidate if he is not sure what to do. This is another occasion when a few words to the candidate before the ceremony can enhance his confidence on what is about to happen and what he will be required to do – he is there to enjoy his ceremony as much as possible. You then lead him to the lodge room door and direct him to salute the Master prior to leaving the lodge, and then return to your seat after he has left; this may be directly or by doing a complete circuit of the room as required by your lodge traditions.

When the candidate re-enters the lodge room for either a second or third degree, he will usually be under the supervision of the Senior Deacon, so your job is to adjust the kneeling cushion or stool as required. After the candidate has regained his feet, you remove this and place it out of the way for the two or three perambulations, and you either return to your seat or you follow the procession if that is the preferred modus operandi of your lodge. If the latter, it may be better that the Inner Guard tidies away the kneeler once you have moved it aside, as to be left too far behind the candidate initially would not look very aesthetically pleasing.

As the Senior Deacon is going to guide the candidate to the East by the appropriate movements, your next job is to appear at the left side of the candidate as he arrives at the Master's pedestal. This will take a little thought if you are not in the procession, and you may decide to set off from your place smartly in order to arrive punctually, or you may elect to glide quietly and slowly to be close to the East for a final acceleration as the candidate arrives. It would be worth checking the best approach with your senior colleague or the Director of Ceremonies at a practice, so that you feel confident about the most efficient method. Some lodges permit the Junior Deacon temporarily to occupy the Senior Deacon's seat so that he is already in the East, and only has a short distance to move to rejoin his colleague and the candidate in front of the Master.

In the second degree you are required to hold a working tool with which to support the candidate's arm, and often the Master will hand it to you or it will be left ready for you on the kneeling stool. With a wand and a working tool in each hand it is obvious that you will not be holding any additional sign during the obligation, and you remove the working tool before the candidate seals his obligation, possibly returning it to the Master. In the second degree you will then return to your seat while the candidate is having the signs, token and word explained and demonstrated to him, or you will stay with him until he is invested with his apron – as this is in the West of the lodge you will then be close to your seat anyway.

For the third degree you again appear at the Master's pedestal for the obligation, but this time you can hold the appropriate sign whilst crossing wands during the obligation, as there is no implement to apply to the candidate. You stay in the East after the obligation until the Wardens take over, at which juncture you retire to your seat or take up a position to the rear of the floor cloth for a short time before sitting down. In both degree ceremonies your work is now finished, because the Senior Deacon will escort the candidate out of the lodge room and will supervise his re-entry. Even though you do not participate in the ceremony further, it is worth noting how the Senior Deacon conducts the candidate around the lodge room thereafter, as in the following year this will be your job. While you will doubtless have watched the ceremonies several times before, there is an increased level of awareness with the immediacy of your stepping into the next lodge office.

Compared to all of your responsibilities during an initiation, in the other two ceremonies you only play a supporting role, in the second degree after you have guided the candidate through the question and answer session. You will need to know how much the Deacons act as a pair or independently, and the timing for when you have to link up again with the Senior Deacon during any part of the ceremonies after he has been working alone. If you have mastered the first degree ceremony, you will have little difficulty in coping with the others, even as Senior Deacon when it becomes your time to move on.

Other Lodge Business

You are often back on your feet almost immediately the ceremony is completed, in order to take the charity collection, and it looks well-rehearsed if you have already agreed with the Senior Deacon – if both of you are involved – which sides of the lodge room you will cover. It always looks somewhat more dignified if you both rise together, set off from the Secretary's table together before and return simultaneously after the collection, and then sit down together – you give the appearance of a well-drilled team. In some lodges the collection is included in the initiation ceremony, but you will already be aware of this if it is; other lodges take the collection as a separate item, and yet others take it during the closing ode or hymn. You then assist in closing the lodge as above, with the added caveat that you may need to collect the working tools used in the ceremony and replace them in their box in the process. If any visitor, in tendering greetings to the Master, alludes to the quality of your work in the lodge, then accept it gracefully because it not only reflects on you but also on your lodge that taught you, and it was obviously well-merited.

Among the other items of business that the Deacons are often involved with are ballots, whether for candidates, joining brethren, or for the Master Elect, Treasurer and Tyler for the ensuing year. As you are supporting the Senior Deacon, greater detail is contained in the next section. Many lodges have the Deacons distribute everything and collect everything, sometimes with three or more circuits of the lodge room in so doing; others request the members to come to the Secretary's table in order to exercise their right to take part in the ballot, which can be more efficient but may be dependent on the size of the lodge room available.

Installations and Visitations

At the installation, as well as on other high days and holidays, you may have to escort one or more senior Masons into and out of the lodge room. The Provincial Grand Master, his Deputy and Assistants will often merit the presence of the Provincial Director of Ceremonies or one of his Deputies, and sometimes they insist on two Provincial Officers acting as Deacons for these entrances and departures, in which case you can relax. However, if you are required, then the lodge Director of Ceremonies or his Provincial equivalent will explain exactly where he wants you and when, and it looks best if the two Deacons can carry their wands at the same height, even if you are of different stature – team working again. You will normally lead in the procession, which will form two columns behind you, then the Deacons both stand aside to let the columns past and afterwards you walk down between those columns as an immediate escort to the most senior Mason attending, and step aside at the end of the columns to let him through. An alternative arrangement is for the Deacons to lead the procession to the East of the lodge room, face inwards with the two columns to let the senior Mason through, and he is then followed by all of the other processing Masons in order of seniority. Either way, you now wait until everyone else has sat down, or if retiring until they have all left the lodge room (crossing wands as they exit), and then you return to your seats after a nod from the Director of Ceremonies.

One further item of note is that often the two Deacons will be invested together in the installation proceedings, as the addresses are very similar, and both are escorted to their seats and they then can sit down in unison. The only other item for the new Junior Deacon to remember at an installation is that, when tidying up the lodge room during the closing, there may be all three sets of working tools to be replaced in the box, and while throwing them in a heap is time-saving, to replace them properly only takes a little longer and looks very much smarter – another example of 'a place for everything and everything in its place'.

If you are moving from Junior to Senior Deacon you may have a slight sense of *déjà vu*, but in some ways the lodge room takes on a completely different perspective, quite literally, when you are looking at it for the first time from the North East. No matter, a little time to re-orient yourself while the other Officers are being collared is well spent, and don't forget that the new Junior Deacon may well be looking at you very keenly for guidance, because for him the

Line drawing of Antiquity's jewels. An early illustration of the Deacons' Mercury jewels as used by Lodge of Antiquity No 2, London, showing a slight variation between the Senior (left) and Junior Deacons' jewels (right), both without a book.

The Senior Deacon's jewel of Enoch Lodge No 11, London, showing one of the variations in the old designs depicting Mercury.

Deacon's collar and wand jewels from Marquis of Granby Lodge No 124, Durham. Several lodges in the North East of England still use the sun and moon jewels, but unusually in this case the sun represents the Senior Deacon and the moon the Junior Deacon – in other lodges the jewels are reversed. Interestingly, in the USA the Deacons also use sun and moon jewels, set in the square and compasses, but the American lodges have adopted the Marquis of Granby's allocation of the sun to the Senior and the moon to the Junior Deacons.

The Senior Deacon

Y ou have arrived at this office from the junior equivalent – so you have seen it all, done it all, and got the tee-shirt to prove it. This office will be a breeze, a few different words and actions here and there, but the hard work has been done and the basics are already instilled into your memory banks. It all sounds easy, and indeed it is, so this is an office when you really can enjoy the benefits of your earlier labours in learning the role of Junior Deacon. With this confidence, remember the new Deacon will gratefully accept your guidance if it is needed, so be watching out for him in the first degree as well as for your candidate in the other two.

Of course, with these days of sometimes dwindling lodge memberships and low levels of recruitment, you may have had a very quiet year as Junior Deacon, and then suddenly as Senior Deacon an influx of new members means you are operating at full throttle. In these circumstances you may need to make a rapid advancement in Masonic knowledge, although it is likely that at the practice meetings as Junior Deacon you will have run through one or two ceremonies, so that the lodge is prepared for the arrival of a candidate when he comes forward. As before, you have a few short passages to say at the appropriate times, but your main function is to escort the candidates to wherever the next presentation will be made to them. By way of a bonus, the candidate for passing and raising already has an inkling of what is to come from his first ceremony, so the escorting aspect should be easier than you previously or your current fellow Deacon might have had to contend with.

An Outline of the Duties

When you are appointed and invested at the installation meeting, your duties will be explained to you, and in all probability this will be done in conjunction with the Junior Deacon whose responsibilities and duties are similar to yours. The main differences between the two sets of duties are that you act as a messenger between the Master and the Senior Warden and attend on candidates during their passing and raising and, although unstated it is also expected that you will assist in the ceremony of initiation where appropriate. You have moved places in the lodge room, however, because you are now seated in the East near the Master, whilst the Junior Deacon is at the opposite end of the lodge room next to the Senior Warden.

First Business of the Lodge

Your first duty at a normal lodge meeting will possibly be to escort the Master and Wardens to their places in the lodge room and then to assist in opening the lodge. The directions are as explained for the Junior Deacon: preceding the Principal Officers to each pedestal in turn, and then accompanying the Director of Ceremonies as far as your seat, and then answering the Master with regard to your place in the room and your duties if required. Thereafter you will need to attend to the tracing boards, possibly escort the Immediate Past Master to formally open the Book in the East, and perhaps be involved in lighting the candles at the three pedestals, all in conformity with your lodge protocol. When the lodge closes, you simply reverse the order of entering the lodge and leave the room preceding the Master or forming a guard of honour immediately in front of the lodge room door.

Your next action normally occurs with the minutes of the previous regular lodge meeting. If the Master alone signs the minutes of the previous meeting as a true record, then either you or the Secretary will carry the minute book to him; you may or may not require your wand, depending on the preference of your lodge. If the minutes are signed by the Wardens as well, then you may carry the minutes around the lodge room yourself or you may combine with the Junior Deacon to do so. Again your lodge will have a preference for you squaring the room formally or walking directly to your destination, and if the former you may also have to salute the Wardens as you pass them. It may also be a lodge tradition that, if there is a senior Provincial representative present at a meeting such as the installation, he is also invited to sign the minute book. If this is the case, after the Wardens have signed you would return to the Master's pedestal, because in all probability the senior Mason will be seated to the North of the Master, and he can sign the minute book as well and you can then return it to the Secretary.

Escorting Candidates

First Degree
In an initiation ceremony, you will make your way round the lodge room to pick up the Junior Deacon, who will go to the lodge room door, whilst you either accompany him or adjust the kneeling cushion/stool and wait there as appropriate. You can help to steady the candidate whilst he is kneeling either here or in the East, but remember there is no sign required from the candidate during this prayer, unlike in the other ceremonies. Once the candidate is on his feet again you will normally be responsible for moving the kneeling cushion/stool out of the way, and then either accompanying the procession or returning to your seat, whichever is required. If the latter you will rejoin the

candidate on his left side at the Master's pedestal, where it will be your job to ensure that the candidate holds the required instrument in his left hand, and you must ensure he hands it back at the end of the obligation, which you hand over to the Master or someone else in the East. If you cross wands with the Junior Deacon and possibly the Director of Ceremonies, then remember to hold the wand in your left hand as you should be standing to order with your right.

You may then leave the Junior Deacon to attend to the candidate on his own, or you may continue to accompany the candidate until he leaves the lodge room, and if the latter you will be playing the supporting role. In fact the initiation ceremony is much more fun if you have two candidates, because it keeps you busy for the whole time rather than playing only bit-parts, but not many lodges enjoy this luxury these days. When the candidate re-enters the lodge room after dressing, it is normal for the Junior Deacon to perform the escort duties alone. When the proceedings are over, in some lodges the initiate is placed in the North East and often next to the Senior Deacon, so welcome him with a smile of congratulations – you will be the first person after the Master to be able to welcome him into lodge membership, and after about an hour of concentration he will doubtless be ready to sit down.

Second Degree
Presentation
For the passing of candidates, you take charge of them when they re-enter the lodge and, if you do not proceed directly to the door of the lodge, you will go round the lodge to pick up the Junior Deacon so that he can attend to the kneeling cushion/stool. You wait for the test by the Inner Guard on the candidate and then lead him to the North West or West of the lodge room for the prayer. This time the candidate knows about the signs during prayers, so you just ensure he complies with tradition.

Then you start the perambulations of the lodge, and sometimes Deacons are confused as to how many tours of the room are required. The sequence always includes one perambulation to present the candidate as prepared for the coming ceremony, so the initiate has his one tour. Before that in the other degrees, there are additional perambulations for the candidate to demonstrate his knowledge of the degrees he has already gone through, so there is one prior tour for the Entered Apprentice ready for passing and two for the Fellowcraft about to be raised. The total number of perambulations therefore equals the number of the degree to be performed, but you must remember to halt in the North West before commencing the final tour, because the Master announces that the candidate is now being formally presented for the forthcoming degree.

For passing or raising you first ensure the candidate salutes the Master as he crosses in front of the pedestal, either in passing or by stopping to salute. You then formally present him to the Wardens, using almost exactly the words that the Tyler and Inner Guard have already used in their announcements of the candidate. The candidate may be surprised when you pronounce the words in their entirety, as previously he has carefully split them as instructed, so be prepared for a hesitation in his repeating them. After the pass grip and password, you then ensure the candidate is facing East while the Senior Warden formally presents him to the Master.

Obligation and Demonstration

Remember that it is the Senior Warden and not the Master who directs you to escort the candidate to the East, and in some lodges the Deacons turn to salute him when they are addressed. You place the candidate towards the centre of the lodge so that he can see you demonstrate perhaps the most difficult mime in the ritual book, which needs some style in order to make the manoeuvre have any decorum. Some lodges roll out a sheet with a winding staircase depicted, otherwise you need to pick your feet up slightly to create the illusion of ascending. In most lodges there are five forward steps and then a half-step to bring the feet together again, but in other lodges they count to five differently. You may then have to retrace your steps down the staircase, which is by walking normally, and then take the candidate through the same procedure, either walking with him and enacting the same climb, or by walking alongside him. Ensure he finishes close to the kneeling stool, and hopefully your brother Junior Deacon has arrived at the pedestal with you.

The candidate is settled on the stool and you cross wands, but during the obligation let the Master request any corrections in the candidate's repetition of the words; the candidate is under his direct supervision and he will decide the importance of absolute correctness. After noting the position of the square and compasses, in this degree the Master proceeds immediately into the entrusting of the signs, token and word, and he will do this with the candidate in front of him, to the side of the pedestal, or on the lodge room floor as appropriate. Again the candidate is under the supervision of the Master, but he may need prompting how to start any action requested of him. You should also have seen the candidate beforehand to explain that, when you are dictating the answers to the Master's or Wardens' questions, you expect him to wait before replying and then to repeat what you have said. This should save you from trying to restrain his enthusiasm inside the lodge, which is always commendable but makes your life complicated.

You next conduct the candidate to the Wardens, introduce him, and then dictate the answers he should give – just as the Master has instructed you to do. There is only one long word in the responses to the Senior Warden, and it is worth saying it slowly as a single word, as it can be difficult for the candidate to decipher it if rattled off as part of a long phrase. Hopefully you will be lettering the word spelled out by the Master with the Junior Warden and halving it with the Senior Warden, but lodges have their own traditions in this respect. After the interchanges with the Wardens, the Senior

Warden presents the candidate for investiture of his new apron, which you may need to assist him with, especially as the normal procedure calls for the fitting of the new apron before the removal of the previous one. For the presentation you will hand the candidate to the Senior Warden and then stand to the North of them, all facing East.

Explanation
Remember that the Master immediately follows up the investiture with a few additional comments, so do not set off for the East at once or your over-eagerness will be out of place. You then position the candidate in the South East, perhaps with his feet around the perfect ashlar, and direct his attention to the next remarks by the Master, and afterwards you may need to place him elsewhere for the explanation of the working tools. Following this you take the candidate to the door of the lodge in order to retire, and guide him through the three-part sign which he may still not be used to.

When he returns the Tyler should have practised the sign with the candidate, in which case it will be a more confident candidate who returns to salute the Master. The placing of the candidate for the explanation of the tracing board will depend on where this is situated. On the floor, on a table top, against the Senior Warden's pedestal, in a free-standing tracing board rack, or on the wall behind curtains are a few variations, so the form and furniture of the lodge room will to some extent dictate where you position the candidate. The explanation may be the long or short variation but, if you remain at the candidate's side for this, remember to prompt the candidate at the end to come to order with the correct sign.

You may also be required to conduct the candidate for the second degree charge, possibly given by the Senior Warden, and then either you escort the candidate to the Master to be congratulated or directly to a seat in the lodge room – possibly adjacent to yours, when you and he can finally relax.

Third Degree
Presentation

With the ceremony of raising, the candidate is under your jurisdiction from the commencement until the Wardens take over for a brief period, after which he completes the ceremony with you again. It is again well worthwhile having a short chat with the candidate before the meeting starts, so that he not only has confidence in you but is prepared for the format of the ceremony and he is aware when he should wait for a prompt from you. For the ceremony you start by collecting the candidate so that he can answer the test questions, which is normally done from the West or centre of the lodge room. You then conduct him to the Master for entrusting with the test of merit, ensuring that he repeats the Master's words if he seems reluctant or slow to do so. You then escort him to the door to allow him to exit, after saluting the Master appropriately.

After the lodge is opened in the third degree, you and the Junior Deacon may be required to prepare the floor cloth for the next part of the ceremony, which may be left rolled up in the centre of the lodge or be opened out to reveal its design. You should not need your wand for this activity, but you will have discussed the methodology with your Junior Deacon, as it looks amateurish to be sorting out what is required during the ceremony rather than being a well-practised team going smoothly about its business. Then when the candidate is announced you will go to collect him, and remember that the lights in the lodge will be extinguished as you proceed to the door, preferably just before it is opened. You will need to take care that your eyes become adjusted before you place the candidate before the kneeling stool, or your first reminder of its presence may be you or the candidate tripping over it!

You then start on two circuits of the Principal Officers, and it should be easy to recall that you demonstrate the first degree information on the first circuit to the Junior Warden, and that of the second degree on the second circuit to the Senior Warden. You then halt in the North West, facing East, because the Master will introduce the final perambulation. This is mostly similar to those that have preceded it, but watch out for the gentleman of metals; there is every sympathy for the candidate saying his profession incorrectly, but the lodge will be waiting expectantly to hear you pronounce it properly – black mark if you fail!

Obligation and Demonstration
The Senior Warden then directs you to take the candidate to the East, and you lead him to a position to watch your demonstration of the proper method. It is usual that there are a final four forward steps and then the feet are brought together, but again each lodge has its own traditions. You then lead the candidate to copy your example, and it is very difficult to walk with him as you might have done in the second degree, so this is a time to point out where you want his feet to go by indicating with your wand; you may walk the final four steps with him. If you are short in stature you may find the demonstration of the Emulation directions on how to place your feet somewhat painful: doing the splits with the feet a distance apart sideways and lengthways, and with the feet ending up pointing in opposite directions, is definitely for contortionists. More importantly, however, even if you want to show off your prowess but the candidate himself is short in stature, you should in fairness demonstrate a technique of advancing that he can emulate.

The Master then conducts the obligation and alludes to the position of the square and compasses again, and will then start on the retrospect of previous ceremonies. Before he does so, you may need to adjust the candidate's position back from the pedestal, depending on whether or not the Master usually leaves his seat for the later enactment. If you do move backwards, it will usually be to the edge of the floor cloth. When the Wardens approach, there is often a short procedure for them replacing the Deacons; perhaps by a pause after the hand on the shoulder, a sideways step by both Deacons in unison, the Wardens advancing, holding the line of five for a moment, and the Deacons retreating. You may go back to your seats or to the rear of the floor cloth, depending on your later role in the ceremony. Indeed, if the floor cloth is still rolled up, you and the Junior Deacon will need to unroll it, and again a smooth working in tandem makes for an efficient operation being performed.

Even if you are positioned at the rear of the floor cloth, your role will only be one of a watching brief; the Master and Wardens will enact this part of the ceremony. After the Wardens depart, the Master or another Past Master will take the candidate through the signs, token and words. You may be required to adjust the candidate's left hand, as the person demonstrating cannot see if this part of the signs is being done correctly. You then collect the candidate, but on this occasion there is no demonstration circuit of the Wardens for him to display the new information to them. You therefore conduct him round to exit the lodge, first saluting the Master with the appropriate signs before leaving the room.

On the candidate's return you have to lead him through the full signs of the third degree, and hopefully the Tyler will have had the candidate practise them in full. After this there is an immediate wheel to give the candidate's hand to the Senior Warden for him to present him to the Master and then invest him with his Master Mason's apron. You will be able to assist in the removal of the Fellowcraft's apron as well as in passing the strap of the new apron round the back of the candidate. You collect him from the Senior Warden, and then wait with him for the Master's remarks on the significance of the apron.

Explanation
The candidate then has the traditional history explained to him, and you place him appropriately at the Master's pedestal or

elsewhere for this to happen. You may be expected to stay with him, or you may return to your seat. As he has several signs to emulate during the history, it is probably better if you stay with him because, of all of the degree signs, it is in the third degree that the candidate is tempted to act as a mirror image of the demonstrator rather than using his correct hand. Although the person demonstrating can keep correcting the candidate, if this happens frequently it is possible that he may begin to lose the continuity of his explanation, and a Deacon gently advising the candidate can be very beneficial.

The explanation of the working tools forms the end of the traditional history and will probably be given wherever the rest of the history has been delivered, even if it is another member of the lodge who explains their significance. If the charge after raising is also given, then this again will normally need no further movement of the candidate, who will probably then be congratulated by the Master on his raising, after which both you and he can sit down and take a well-earned rest.

Other Lodge Business

The Deacons are usually involved with any ballots that take place (and some lodges still ballot for initiates on the evening of their induction), either using black and white balls for candidates or slips of paper for the annual election of the Master Elect and Treasurer. Your lodge probably has a well-rehearsed routine for doing this, and if you have seen it many times before then you will merely enact a repeat of what you have seen. With ballots it is courtesy to hand out the first items to the Master and then the senior lodge members (remembering that honorary members do not vote) in the East, and then to work around the lodge room to other members and the Officers, not forgetting the Tyler outside the door if he wishes to vote. You should hand out one ball of each colour to every member; if the members are left to make their own selection they may inadvertently do so incorrectly. If the ballot box has 'yes' and 'no' drawers, then one colour ball only is required.

Remember to let the Master see the empty ballot box before starting the collection of votes, to ensure that none of the wrong kind has been left inside by mistake. Collection of the ballot, and afterwards collecting the balls left over, is performed in the same order as issuing them, and in all likelihood you as Senior Deacon will present the Master with the ballot box for him to be able to announce the result to the lodge. You will stand to one side while he reports the result, and then collect the box and present it to the Wardens if required or return it directly to the Secretary's table. Also remember to collect the unused ballot balls in the same ballot box, so that the balls are all mixed together – this second collection is just as private as the initial voting was. If both Deacons are involved, remember that it looks better if you both sit down in your seats together.

In the paper ballots for the Master Elect and Treasurer, the Deacons initially hand out two slips of paper to each member. The Master explains the lodge tradition in such elections and what qualifications are required of candidates for the Master Elect. The Senior Deacon collects the slips for the first ballot for Master Elect and hands the ballot box to the Master who then sifts through the votes, often assisted by one or two senior lodge members. He formally announces the outcome of the ballot, and the Master Elect suitably responds. The Senior Deacon then collects the ballot papers for the election of the Treasurer and a similar procedure is followed, with the Senior Deacon sitting down after handing the ballot box to the Master as before.

The other item of business involving the Senior Deacon is the presentation of a Grand Lodge certificate. You will normally be called on to escort the Master Mason to the centre of the lodge or near the Secretary's table, and another member of the lodge may go through a full or partial explanation of its format and usage. The recipient is afterwards asked to sign his certificate at the Secretary's table, and you may then be expected to escort him to the Master who will check the certificate has been completed satisfactorily before congratulating him. You then escort him back to his seat in the lodge and return to your own. If more than one person is receiving a certificate at a lodge meeting, the Junior Deacon may be called on to accompany the second recipient, otherwise you will escort the first person and request the others to follow you and him.

Installations and Visitations
These duties have already been outlined for the Junior Deacon, and there are no aspects that are different for the Senior Deacon, as you operate as a team on these occasions. The only change is that instead of you as Junior Deacon possibly requiring advice from your senior partner, as Senior Deacon you should be the one giving advice based on your additional experience. Also if it is the lodge tradition for the Junior Deacon to attend to the tracing boards, etc., you will be holding his wand while he does so during the opening and closing ceremonies rather than vice versa. Because of your position towards the East of the lodge, you may also find yourself holding the wand of a Provincial Director of Ceremonies while he leads the salutes to the visiting dignitaries.

   If you are progressing towards the Chair of King Solomon, then this will be the last year that you are a junior Officer, as your next role will be as one of the Principal Officers of the lodge. You will be instructing the junior Officers to carry out their duties, so you will now have the chance to develop the relationship between Principals and Assistant Officers from the other end of the spectrum. Remember the adage: 'It's nice to be important, but it's more important to be nice.' You were once a junior reporting to a senior colleague, so recall how you were occasionally assisted by him when necessary and without undue fuss, and similarly try to help your junior colleagues as appropriate.

A Check List for Laying Out the Lodge Room

This is primarily for the Tyler and Director of Ceremonies, and can be adapted as necessary, but your lodge layout may contain the following:

Master's pedestal – has cushion, closed Book (with bookmarks in appropriate places), square and compasses, gavel, gauntlets, heavy maul and summons in place.

Senior Warden's pedestal – has cushion, Doric column – horizontal, gavel, gauntlets, level.

Junior Warden's pedestal – has cushion, Corinthian column – vertical, gavel, gauntlets, plumb rule.

Deacons', Director of Ceremonies' and his Assistant's seats – the correct holders for the respective wands are in place (and they may be of different diameters), and also the wands if appropriate.

Inner Guard's seat – has poignard, and square or compasses as appropriate, for use during the entry of the candidates.

Secretary's and Treasurer's table – spare summons, lodge items, collection plates or bags, minute book, pedestal for reading, lodge by-laws, Book of Constitutions for reading of an ancient charge (if required) and regulations for the Master Elect at an installation, lodge ritual for reference, etc.

Tyler's seat – has sword and summons, Tyler's book or signing-in sheets on a table adjacent to the entrance door, and clothing for the candidate if required.

Other Tyler's items – can include sticking plasters (to cover rings and earrings), stout rubber bands (in case the candidate's feet are much smaller than the slipper or slipshod), a torch if required in one of the ceremonies (and for power cuts), lighter or matches for the candles, as well as spare white gloves and black tie in case any visitor – and indeed any member – has forgotten these items, etc.

Ancient Charge – or Book of Constitutions placed for whoever is reading an ancient charge during the opening of the meeting.

Ashlars – to be placed appropriately; the rough one with the Junior Warden or in the North East corner of the square pavement; the perfect ashlar with the Senior Warden or in the South East corner, and the latter ashlar may be mounted under a tripod.

Ballot box and balls – placed on Secretary's table if there is a ballot; ballot slips if there is a written election.

Banner – displayed in lodge room.

Candles – to be checked that they will light, with matches, taper or electricity as appropriate; place matches and taper ready for use (some lodges begin with candles already lit, others have a short ceremony to light them); if electric candles check they are plugged in and the bulbs work.

Hymn sheets – on all seats or by entrance door (the Secretary, Treasurer and Organist will usually look after their own paperwork themselves).

Lectern – in position or ready to be moved into position if there is a lecture; often a job for the Deacons or Inner Guard.

Memorabilia – there may be items donated to the lodge by members or visitors that are to be displayed at meetings, for example on the Secretary's table, as well as other lodge furniture such as gongs, etc.

Mourning – pedestals and Secretary's table draped appropriately; black bows on columns and wands; black rosettes on Officers' collars and for other lodge members; a period of mourning may be decreed by Grand Lodge or Provincial Grand Lodge, or it may be caused by the death of a lodge member.

Officers' collars and aprons – on appropriate seats or in the anteroom.

Ordering meals – count up the number of signatures in the Tyler's book, and check if the Director of Ceremonies has included the initiate(s) if it is a first degree ceremony.

Pointer – placed close by the tracing board to be explained if required.

Tracing Boards – if movable, placed appropriately round room and, if nested together, ensure they are in the correct order.

Visitor cards – will assist the Inner Guard to announce visitors and latecomers if the need arises; should be with the Tyler's book or signing-in sheets.

Wands – to be placed in appropriate stands, or by the door of the lodge if it is customary to process in; doves, Mercuries or sun/moon for the Deacons and crossed wands for the DC and ADC (in some lodges the DC has a baton).

Warrant – displayed in lodge room.

Working tools – placed appropriately for presentation.

Initiation – blindfold, cable tow and slipper near Tyler's seat; declaration book and collection plate at Secretary's table; Entered Apprentice apron at Master's or Senior Warden's pedestal; first degree tools at Master's or Junior Warden's pedestal; Book of Constitutions and lodge by-laws at the Master's pedestal.

Passing – slipper near Tyler's seat; square at Inner Guard's seat; Fellow Craft apron at Master's or Senior Warden's pedestal; second degree tools at Master's or Senior Warden's pedestal.

Raising – 2 slippers near Tyler's seat; compasses at Inner Guard's seat; floor cloth and emblems of mortality for Deacons to lay out; torch for a Past Master to use; Master Mason apron at Master's or

Senior Warden's pedestal (previously check for fit on candidate); third degree tools at Master's pedestal.

Installation – all sets of working tools and list of new Officers at Master's pedestal; Book of Constitutions and lodge by-laws at Secretary's table or appropriately placed; hanger for Officers' collars when handed in; all collars to be worn or in the lodge room ready for investiture (covers absent brethren).

However reliable your Director of Ceremonies and Tyler are, it is advisable for each Officer of the lodge to check that he has all of his required equipment for the business of the meeting, as this will avoid a temporary halt to the proceedings if a necessary item is missing at the appropriate juncture.

Order of Appointing and Investing Officers and Their Respective Jewels

(also useful for laying out collars on the chairs occupied by the respective Officers)

Worshipful Master . . . . square (elected not appointed)
Immediate Past Master . . . . square and problem (not appointed)
Senior Warden . . . . level
Junior Warden . . . . plumb rule
Chaplain . . . . open book on a triangle
Treasurer . . . . key (elected, not appointed)
Secretary . . . . two crossed pens/quills
Director of Ceremonies . . . . . . two crossed wands
Almoner . . . . purse bearing a heart
Charity Steward . . . . trowel
Senior Deacon . . . . dove and olive branch, or Mercury/sun/moon
Junior Deacon . . . . dove and olive branch, or Mercury/moon/sun
Assistant Director of Ceremonies two crossed wands and word 'Assistant'
Organist . . . . lyre
Assistant Secretary . . . . two crossed pens/quills and word 'Assistant'
Inner Guard . . . . two crossed swords
Steward . . . . cornucopia
Tyler . . . . vertical sword

Further Reading

There are many books and papers that go into more detail about topics necessarily covered very briefly in this book. There are two relatively recent Prestonian lectures that discuss the historical aspects of the Tyler (and Inner Guard) and the Deacons and were published under the auspices of Ars Quattuor Coronati (AQC):

1977: Roy A. Wells, *'The Tyler or Outer Guard'*;
1985: Sinclair Bruce, *'...not only Ancient but useful and necessary Officers...the Deacons'*.

For those wanting to learn more about the different versions of the Craft ritual, Lewis Masonic produces several books, including the Emulation, Logic, Oxford, Sussex, Taylor's, Universal and West End workings. These and other books and rituals for freemasons are available from Lewis Masonic Mail Order Dept, 4 Watling Drive, Hinkley, Leics LE10 3EY. Please send or telephone for our catalogue (Tel 01455 254450).

Acknowledgements

I would like to thank those members of the Brigantes' Ritual Working Party who assisted in the proof reading and commented on the draft of this book, and a special thanks to James Abbott of Brigantes Lodge 9734 and Tim Smith of Gild of St Mary Lodge 7288 and several lodges for providing/allowing photographs of the Officers' jewels, as well as placing on record – as ever – the patience of my wife Linda while I was immersed in researching for and compiling this book.